iOS 18
User Manual

User Guide for Tricks, Tips, New Features, and All You Need to Know about Enhanced Features of iOS 18

By

Tatiana Dash

Disclaimer:

Table of Contents

iOS 18, What's In It? 5

    Makes iPhone More Personal, Capable, And More Intelligent. 5

    New Customization and Capability 6

    Photos Get a Unified View, New Customization and Collections. 7

    Great Ways to Stay Connected in Messages 8

    Enhancements to Mail...9

    Big Updates to Safari 10

    Introducing the Passwords App...14

Getting Started 15

  Updating to iOS 18 15

  Set Up Your Device on iOS 18...17

    Tips for a Smooth Setup 21

  Basics of the iOS 18 Interface 21

Interface and Navigation 28

  Home Screen and Widgets 28

    Customize the Home Screen 28

    Use and Organize Widgets 32

    App Library Overview 36

  Control Center and Notifications 41

    Access and Customize the Control Center 41

    Manage Notifications 45

    Notification Summary and Scheduling 51

  Gestures and Multitasking 55

    Essential Gestures for Navigation 55

    Use Multitasking Features..61

    Switching Between Apps 64

  Spotlight and Siri 68

Use Spotlight Search 68

Enhancements to Siri and Voice Commands in iOS 18 71

Siri Shortcuts and Automation 74

Core Apps and Features 79

Messages and FaceTime 79

New Features in Messages for iOS 18 79

Enhancements in FaceTime for iOS 18 83

Use SharePlay and Other Collaboration Tools 85

Settings and Customization 89

General Settings 89

Overview of the Settings App 89

Device Management and Information 92

Accessibility Features 95

Privacy and Security 97

Enhanced Privacy Settings in iOS 18 97

Advanced Features 101

Cloud and Storage Management 101

App Store and App Management 103

Health and Fitness 105

Connectivity and Integration 109

Connect with Other Devices 109

Home and Smart Devices 111

CarPlay and External Displays 113

Troubleshooting and Maintenance 116

Common Issues and Solutions 116

iOS 18, What's In It?

Longed-for iOS 18? It is the latest evolution in Apple's quest to deliver an exceptional mobile experience. This update brings a host of innovative features and enhancements, designed to make your iPhone more powerful, personal, and secure. Here's a glimpse of what iOS 18 has to offer:

Makes iPhone More Personal, Capable, And More Intelligent.

The much-awaited iOS 18, Apple said, makes the iPhone more personal and more intelligent than you have ever seen. Unveiling this "wonder" operating system the company said it incorporates new customization options, and described it as "the biggest-ever redesign of Photos, powerful updates for staying connected, and Apple Intelligence, the personal intelligence system."

iPhone devices as shown display a customized Home Screen, enhanced Tapbacks in Messages, and the redesigned Photos app, as available.

This OS has surely introduced fresh ways of customizing the iPhone, plus additional ways to stay connected in Messages, and more.

While promoting the new iOS 18, Apple said that it features new ways for users to manage their inboxes in Mail and Messages over satellite. Users can arrange apps and widgets in any open space on the Home Screen, customize the buttons at the bottom of the Lock Screen, and rapidly access more controls in the Control Center.

Photo libraries will be automatically organized in a new single view in Photos, and accommodating new collections will keep favourites effortlessly accessible. New mail makes simpler the inbox, with on-device intelligence, plus -new text effects in the iMessage. All these are made possible by the same revolutionary technology already existing in iPhone satellite capabilities. You can now conveniently "communicate over satellite in the Messages app when a cellular or Wi-Fi connection isn't available."

That is definitely not all because the new iOS 18 now include **Apple Intelligence**, described as "the personal intelligence system for iPhone, iPad, and Mac that combines the power of generative models with personal context to deliver intelligence that's incredibly useful and relevant."

Built with privacy from the ground up, Apple Intelligence is totally integrated into iOS 18, iPadOS 18, and macOS Sequoia. It ties together the power of Apple silicon to know and generate language and images, take action across apps, and pull from personal context, to make simpler and accelerate daily tasks.

Apple says "We are thrilled to introduce iOS 18. It is a huge release with incredible features," as reported by *Craig Federighi*, Apple's senior vice president of Software Engineering. In *Craig's* words "This release also marks the beginning of a tremendously exciting new era of personal intelligence with Apple Intelligence delivering intuitive, powerful, and instantly useful experiences" that is believed will transform the iPhone experience, with privacy at the core.

New Customization and Capability
You now have fresh ways of customizing your Home Screen, Lock Screen, and Control Center. You can now arrange apps and widgets in open space on the Home Screen, plus the ability to place them right above the dock for easy access or effortlessly framing a wallpaper. App icons and widgets are able to take on a fresh look with a dark or tinted effect, and a user can customize them to appear larger to tailor it to their preferred experience.

Control Center is redesigned to give easier access to many of the things users do on a daily basis, plus its added levels of customization and flexibility. The redesign gives quick access to new groups of a user's most-utilized controls, like media playback, Home controls, and connectivity, including the ability to effortlessly swipe between each. A user will be able to add controls from supported third-party apps into the Control Center to quickly open a vehicle or jump right into capturing content for social media as part of the new feature-all from one place.

The new controls gallery shows the full set of available choices, and a user will be able to customize how the controls display. This includes adjusting them to the preferred size and making entirely new groups.

For the first time, a user can now change the controls at the bottom of the Lock Screen, choose from options available in the controls gallery or take them away entirely. With the **Action button** available on iPhone 15 Pro and iPhone 15 Pro Max, a user will be able to quickly invoke controls available in the gallery.

Jump to other groups of controls.

Photos Get a Unified View, New Customization and Collections.
Photos now have the best-ever redesign to help a user easily locate and relive special moments. A simplified, single view shows the usual grid and new collections that will help a user browse by themes without having to organize content into albums.

Your collections can be pinned to retain your favourites and make them easily accessible. A fresh carousel view presents highlights that update daily and feature preferred people, pets, places, and more.

Auto-playing content throughout the app enlivens libraries so that past moments can be relished while browsing. Note that each user's photo library is unique, the app can be modified also, so that a user can organize collections, pin collections to access them regularly and include what's most vital to them in the carousel view.

Great Ways to Stay Connected in Messages
iMessage gets fresh text effects that "bring conversations to life by amplifying any letter, word, phrase, or emoji with dynamic, animated appearances." A user will be able to better express tone by using formatting such as "bold, underline, italics, and strikethrough." Tapbacks expand to consist of any emoji or sticker, and now a user can write a message and schedule to send it at a later date.

Messages obviously offer more capabilities for self-expression with formatting and animated text effects that you can apply to any letter, word, phrase, or emoji in iMessage. When sending messages to contacts who do not have an Apple device, the Messages app in this feature supports RCS for richer media and more dependable group messaging compared to SMS and MMS.

iOS 18 includes Messages via satellite for the times when cellular and Wi-Fi connections are not readily available. With the help of the same technology that has continued to exist in iPhone satellite capabilities, Messages via satellite will automatically prompt a user "to connect to their nearest satellite right from the Messages app to send and receive texts, emoji, and Tapbacks over iMessage and SMS." With Dynamic Island, a user will always know when they are connected to a satellite, as iMessage was built to protect user privacy, and every iMessage sent via satellite is end-to-end encrypted.

Messages via satellite allows users to send and receive texts, emoji, and

iPhone shows a text conversation in iMessage with a satellite image and the phrase "Keep Pointing at Satellite... Connected" in Dynamic Island.

Enhancements to Mail

Mail brings new ways for users to handle their inboxes and stay up to date. On-device categorization organizes "incoming email into Primary for personal and time-sensitive emails, Transactions for confirmations and receipts, Updates for news and social notifications, and Promotions for marketing emails and coupons." Mail also has a new digest view that puts together all of the relevant emails from a business. This will allow a user to quickly scan for what's important at the moment.

iPhone displays an inbox in Mail with the label Primary shown above a series of emails, and another shows an inbox with multiple emails from United Airlines.

Big Updates to Safari

Safari, the world's fastest browser, now offers an even easier way to find information on the web with Highlights and a restructured Reader experience. Adopting machine learning, Safari will bring up key information about a webpage. For instance, a user can appraise a summary to get the gist of an article, and quickly check the location of a restaurant, hotel, or landmark; or even listen to an artist's track right from an article about the song or album. The reader is also redesigned to give even more ways to enjoy articles without distraction, plus a summary and table of contents for longer articles, and MORE on accessibility and others.

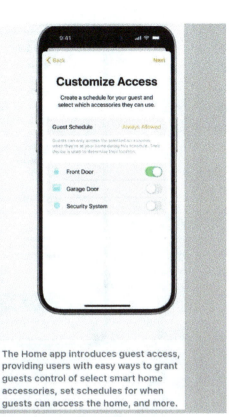

In the Notes app, formulas and equations entered while typing are solved instantly with Math Notes.

The Home app introduces guest access, providing users with easy ways to grant guests control of select smart home accessories, set schedules for when guests can access the home, and more.

. **Summary of the new features and app updates are:**

- **Adaptive User Interface**: You will enjoy a dynamic, responsive UI with themes that adjust automatically based on the time of day and lighting conditions, alongside more interactive widgets right on your Home Screen.

- **Advanced Siri and AI Integration**: You will experience a smarter Siri that offers proactive suggestions based on your daily patterns, and enhanced natural language processing for more accurate responses.

- **Expanded Customization Options**: You will be able to personalize your device like never before with more ways to customize your Home Screen, including custom icon packs and new tools for creating unique lock screens.

- **Enhanced Privacy and Security**: You will protect your data with features like Private Relay for browsing privacy and improved App Privacy Reports that provide real-time alerts on data usage.

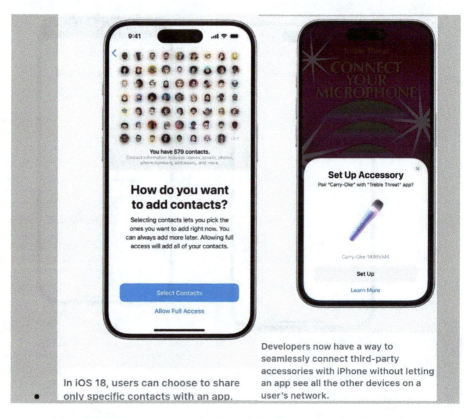

In iOS 18, users can choose to share only specific contacts with an app.

Developers now have a way to seamlessly connect third-party accessories with iPhone without letting an app see all the other devices on a user's network.

- *iPhone displays a screen with the prompt "How do you want to add contacts" and the options "Select Contacts" and "Allow Full Access." another displays an Accessory Setup Kit screen for pairing a microphone with an app called Treble Threat.*

- **Revamped Multitasking and Productivity Tools**: With iOS 18, you will benefit from improved multitasking with Split View and Slide Over, and quick access to notes from anywhere in the system for seamless productivity.

- **Messages**: Enhanced group chat tools and the ability to use live stickers and effects make your conversations more engaging.

- **FaceTime**: Spatial Audio creates an immersive sound experience, and SharePlay enhancements make media sharing and collaboration easier during calls.

- **Photos and Camera**: AI-powered Smart Albums organize your photos effortlessly, while the new Pro Camera Mode offers advanced controls for photography enthusiasts.

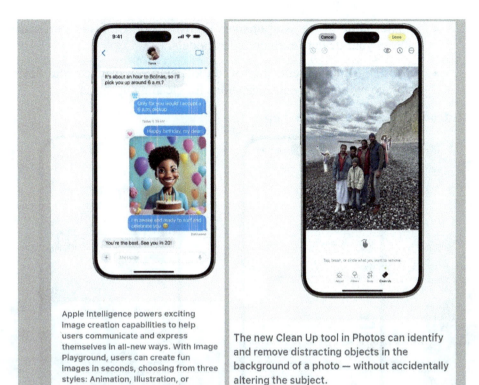

Apple Intelligence powers exciting image creation capabilities to help users communicate and express themselves in all-new ways. With Image Playground, users can create fun images in seconds, choosing from three styles: Animation, Illustration, or Sketch.

The new Clean Up tool in Photos can identify and remove distracting objects in the background of a photo — without accidentally altering the subject.

iPhone displays a text message conversation with an animated birthday image. Another shows Pause playback of video: Clean Up Tool in Photos with Apple Intelligence in iOS 18

- **Safari**: You will be able to organize your browsing with tab groups and enjoy stronger privacy protections with improved tracking prevention.

- **Universal Control**: This will allow you to control and share content across your iPhone, iPad, and Mac seamlessly with a single set of inputs.

- **HomeKit and Smart Device Integration**: Enhanced smart home automation and security make managing your connected devices easier and more secure.

- **Expanded CarPlay Features**: Take advantage of multi-screen support and personalized driving modes tailored to your habits and preferences.

- **Battery Optimization**: Extend your device's battery life with new power management features and insights.

- **Faster and More Responsive**: Enjoy smoother, faster performance across your device, even on older models.

- **Storage Management**: Improved tools help you manage your device's storage with intelligent suggestions for cleaning up space.

Introducing the Passwords App

The new Passwords app makes it easy to access passwords, passkeys, Wi-Fi passwords, and verification codes — all

Locked apps can be hidden in a dedicated folder in the App Library so they don't appear on the Home Screen.

iPhone shows the Passwords app with a list of app icons, including DoorDash, Atlas Obscura, LinkedIn, and more. Another shows the App Library with a dedicated folder for hidden apps.

Perhaps, it is time to upgrade to iOS 18 , with easy steps to back up and migrate your data. Once installed, you'll find guidance on setting up your device and tips on how to explore and take full advantage of the new features.

Getting Started

Updating to iOS 18

Updating your iPhone to iOS 18 is a straightforward process, designed to ensure that you have access to the latest features, security enhancements, and performance improvements. Here's a step-by-step guide to help you smoothly transition to iOS 18:

1. Prepare Your Device

Before starting the update, take these preparatory steps to ensure a smooth process:

- Ensure your iPhone model supports iOS 18. Typically, newer devices are compatible, but it's best to verify this on Apple's official website.

- **Backup Your Data**: It's crucial to back up your device to avoid any potential data loss. You can use iCloud or iTunes (on a computer) to create a complete backup of your device.

   To backup via iCloud:

   o   Go to *Settings > [Your Name] > iCloud > iCloud Backup*.

   o   Tap *Back Up Now* and wait for the process to complete.

   To backup via iTunes/Finder (on a computer):

   o   Connect your iPhone to your computer and open iTunes or Finder.

   o   Select your device, then click *Back Up Now* under the *Summary* tab.

- **Free Up Space**: Ensure you have enough free space for the update. iOS updates typically require a significant amount of storage. You can manage your storage under *Settings > General > iPhone Storage* and remove any unnecessary files or apps.

2. Start the Update

There are two primary methods to update your iPhone to iOS 18: Over the air (OTA) and through a computer.

Updating Over-the-Air (OTA):

1. **Connect to Wi-Fi**: Make sure your iPhone is connected to a stable Wi-Fi network and that it is sufficiently charged or plugged into a power source.

2. **Open Settings**: Navigate to *Settings > General > Software Update*.

3. **Download and Install**: If iOS 18 is available, you'll see an option to *Download and Install*. Tap it, and follow the on-screen instructions to complete the update.

Updating via Computer:

1. **Connect to Your Computer**: Using a USB cable, connect your iPhone to a computer running a compatible version of iTunes (for older macOS or Windows) or Finder (on compatible macOS version).

2. **Select Your Device**: Open iTunes or Finder, select your iPhone, and click on the *Summary* tab.

3. **Check for Update**: Click *Check for Update* and follow the prompts to download and install iOS 18.

3. Complete the Installation

After downloading, your iPhone will need to restart to install iOS 18. This process might take several minutes. During this time, your device will display the Apple logo and a progress bar.

• Your device will automatically restart once the installation is complete. It may go through a few reboot cycles.

• **Follow the Setup Prompts**: After your iPhone restarts, you might see a series of setup screens. Follow these prompts to complete the update process.

4. Post-Update Steps

Once iOS 18 is installed, take these steps to finalize your update:

- **Restore Your Settings and Apps**: Ensure your personal settings, apps, and data are restored correctly from your backup.

- **Explore New Features**: Familiarize yourself with the new features and improvements in iOS 18. The updated interface and new functionalities are designed to enhance user experience.

- **Check App Compatibility**: Make sure all your apps are updated to the latest versions, as some may require updates to function correctly with iOS 18.

5. Troubleshooting Common Issues

If you encounter any problems during or after the update:

- **Restart Your Device**: A simple restart can often resolve minor issues.

- **Check for Software Updates**: Sometimes, Apple releases small updates shortly after a major iOS release to fix bugs. Go to *Settings > General > Software Update* to check for any additional updates.

- **Reset Network Settings**: If you're having connectivity issues, go to *Settings > General > Reset > Reset Network Settings*.

- For persistent problems, visit the Apple Support website or contact an Apple Support representative.

Updating to iOS 18 ensures you have access to the latest features and security updates. Following these steps will help you smoothly transition to the new system, allowing you to take full advantage of all that iOS 18 has to offer

Set Up Your Device on iOS 18

After updating to iOS 18 or you just bought a new iPhone, the initial setup process is designed to get your device ready for use and customized to your preferences. Follow these steps to configure your iPhone and start enjoying the new features of iOS 18:

1. Turn on Your Device

- Press and hold the power button until the Apple logo appears.

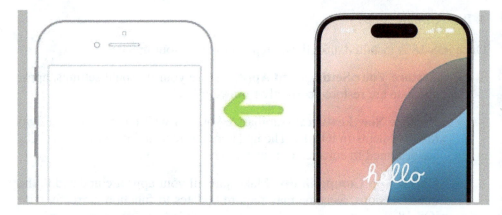

- **Hello Screen**: Once powered on, you'll be greeted by the "Hello" screen in multiple languages. Swipe up to begin the setup process.

2. Select Your Language and Region

- **Language Selection**: Choose your preferred language from the list.

- **Region**: Select your country or region. This setting affects your device's display options for dates, times, and contacts.

3. Connect to Wi-Fi

- Choose a Wi-Fi network from the available options and enter the password to connect. This step is crucial for activating your device and accessing the internet during the setup process.

- **Skip or Use Cellular**: If you don't have access to Wi-Fi, you can use cellular data or skip this step and connect to Wi-Fi later.

4. Activate Your iPhone

- **Activation Process**: Your iPhone will contact Apple's servers to activate. This process may take a few minutes. Ensure you have a stable internet connection.

- **SIM Card**: If you have a SIM card, insert it now to ensure your iPhone can make calls and access mobile data.

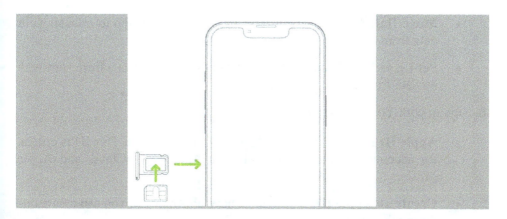

5. Set Up Face ID or Touch ID

- If your device supports Face ID, follow the on-screen instructions to scan your face. This allows you to unlock your phone, authorize payments, and more with facial recognition.

- **Touch ID Setup**: For devices with Touch ID, follow the prompts to scan your fingerprint. This provides similar functionality for unlocking and authorization.

6. Create a Passcode

- **Passcode Security**: Set up a six-digit passcode for additional security. This is required to unlock your device and protect your data.

- **Passcode Options**: You can choose options for a four-digit passcode or a custom alphanumeric code if preferred.

7. Restore or Transfer Your Data

Choose how you want to set up your device:

- **Restore from iCloud Backup**: Select this option if you have a backup on iCloud. Sign in with your Apple ID and choose the latest backup to restore your apps, settings, and data.

- **Restore from Mac or PC**: Connect your iPhone to your computer to restore from a backup stored on iTunes or Finder.

- **Transfer Directly from iPhone**: If you have an old iPhone running iOS 12.4 or later, you can use the Quick Start feature to transfer data wirelessly.

- **Move Data from Android**: Use the *Move to iOS* app to transfer your data from an Android device.

- **Set Up as New iPhone**: Choose this option if you want a fresh start with no data from a previous device.

8. Sign in with Your Apple ID

- **Apple ID Login**: Enter your Apple ID and password. This ID is crucial for accessing Apple services like the App Store, iCloud, and Apple Music.

- **Create an Apple ID**: If you don't have an Apple ID, you can create one during this step.

- **Two-Factor Authentication**: If enabled, verify your identity with the two-factor authentication code sent to your trusted devices or phone number.

9. Set Up Apple Services

- **iCloud**: Configure iCloud to sync and store your data across all Apple devices. You can choose which apps and services to sync.

- **Apple Pay**: Add credit or debit cards to use with Apple Pay for secure, contactless payments.

- **Siri and Voice Recognition**: Enable Siri and set up voice recognition to allow Siri to respond to your commands. You'll be prompted to speak a few phrases to help Siri recognize your voice.

10. Customize Settings and Preferences

- **Location Services**: Enable location services to allow apps like Maps and Find My to access your location.

- **Analytics and Privacy**: Choose whether to share app analytics and diagnostics with Apple to improve products and services.

- **App Permissions**: Set preferences for app permissions, including notifications, location access, and more. You can adjust these settings later in the *Settings* app.

11. Finish Up

- **Display Settings**: Adjust display settings such as True Tone, Night Shift, and screen zoom to your liking.

- **Software Updates**: Check for any additional software updates that might be available post-installation.

- **Welcome to iOS 18**: Once setup is complete, you'll be taken to your Home Screen. From here, you can start exploring the new features and customizing your device further.

12. Explore and Enjoy

- **App Store and Customization**: Visit the App Store to download apps and games. Customize your Home Screen layout and widget settings to suit your preferences.

- Go into the new functionalities and enhancements of iOS 18, such as adaptive themes, advanced multitasking, and improved privacy controls.

Tips for a Smooth Setup

- **Stay Connected**: Keep your device connected to a power source and Wi-Fi during setup to avoid interruptions.

- **Follow the Prompts**: Pay close attention to the setup prompts, as they guide you through essential configurations.

If you encounter issues or have questions, visit the Apple Support website or use the *Apple Support* app.

Basics of the iOS 18 Interface

iOS 18 introduces several refinements and new features to the familiar interface of your iPhone. Understanding the basics of this interface will help you navigate your device more efficiently and make the most of its capabilities. Here's a breakdown of the key elements:

1. Home Screen

Users can choose between a light, dark, or tinted look to create the experience that is perfect for them.

- *iPhone shows app icons and widgets with a dark effect on the Home Screen, and another with a tinted effect on the Home Screen.*

- **Apps and Icons**: The Home Screen displays app icons in a grid layout. You can launch an app by tapping its icon.

- **Dock**: The Dock at the bottom of the screen holds your most frequently used apps, which remain accessible from any Home Screen page.

- **App Library**: Swipe left past the last Home Screen page to access the App Library, which organizes all your apps into automatically generated categories.

2. Widgets and Dynamic Elements

- **Widgets**: Widgets provide at-a-glance information and can be placed on the Home Screen for easy access. You can add, move, and resize widgets by long-pressing the Home Screen and tapping the '+' icon.

- **Dynamic Theme Modes**: The introduction of themes that adapt based on the time of day or environmental lighting, will offer different visual styles that dynamically change throughout the day.

3. Notification Center

- **Access**: Swipe down from the top centre of the screen to open the Notification Center, where you can view and manage recent notifications.

- **Interaction**: Swipe left on a notification to manage it or tap to open the associated app. You can also clear all notifications by pressing and holding the 'X' button and selecting 'Clear All Notifications.'

4. Control Center

- **Access**: Swipe down from the top-right corner (or up from the bottom on older iPhones) to open the Control Center.

- **Quick Controls**: The Control Center provides quick access to essential functions like Wi-Fi, Bluetooth, Airplane Mode, screen brightness, and volume. You can customize Control Center in the *Settings* app under *Control Center*.

Tap to turn on Airplane Mode.

5. App Switcher and Multitasking

- **App Switcher**: Swipe up from the bottom and pause in the middle of the screen (or double-click the Home button on older devices) to access the App Switcher. Here, you can see and switch between recently used apps.

- **Multitasking**: With Split View and Slide Over enhancement on supported devices, you can use two apps side by side or have a floating app overlay.

6. Gestures and Navigation

- **Basic Gestures**:

    o **Tap**: Select an item or app.

    o **Swipe**: Moves between screens or opens features like Notification Center or Control Center.

    o **Pinch**: Zooms in or out in photos, maps, and other apps.

    o **Long Press**: Reveals additional options, like rearranging apps or opening contextual menus.

- **Navigating Without a Home Button**: On newer iPhones without a Home button, swiping up from the bottom returns you to the Home Screen, and swiping left or right along the bottom edge switches between apps.

7. Siri and Search

- **Siri**: Activate Siri by saying "Hey Siri," pressing and holding the side button (or the Home button on older devices), or using the dedicated Siri button in the Control Center. Siri in iOS 18 offers advanced suggestions and more natural interactions.

- **Spotlight Search**: Swipe down from the middle of the Home Screen to access Spotlight Search. Type a query to find apps, contacts, web results, and more.

8. Settings and Personalization

- **Settings App**: Open the *Settings* app to configure your device's options, including network settings, display preferences, notifications, privacy settings, and more.

- **Customization**: Personalize your device with wallpapers, ringtones, app layouts, and widgets. Navigate to *Settings* > *Wallpaper* or long-press the Home Screen to start customizing.

9. Dock and App Organization

- **Dock**: The Dock keeps your most frequently used apps handy at the bottom of the screen. You can add or remove apps from the Dock by dragging them.

- **Folders**: Organize apps into folders by dragging one app icon onto another. This helps keep your Home Screen tidy and makes it easier to find apps.

10. App Library and Searching for Apps

- **App Library**: The App Library automatically organizes all your apps into categories. Access it by swiping left past your Home Screen pages.

- **Search for Apps**: Use the App Library's search bar to quickly find and open apps.

11. Lock Screen and Notifications

- **Lock Screen**: The Lock Screen displays the time, date, and recent notifications. Swipe up to unlock or access the Home Screen (or use Face ID/Touch ID).

- **Notifications**: Notifications appear on the Lock Screen and can be managed by swiping left to open options or right to dismiss.

12. Control Center Customization

Control Center has been redesigned to provide easier access to many of the things users do every day, and it gets new levels of customization

The refreshed design of Control Center delivers quick access to new groups of a user's most-utilized controls

A user can choose between a light, dark, or tinted look to generate the experience that is perfect for them.

- **Customizing Controls**: Go to *Settings > Control Center* to add, remove, or reorder controls for quick access to features like the flashlight, calculator, camera, and more.

13. Tips and Help

- Use the *Tips* app for helpful guides and tutorials on your iPhone and its features.

- **Help and Support**: For more assistance, visit Apple's support website or use the *Apple Support* app.

The new controls gallery displays the full set of available controls

Interface and Navigation

Home Screen and Widgets

Customize the Home Screen

Customizing the Home Screen on iOS 18 allows you to personalize your iPhone's interface to suit your preferences and improve accessibility.

1. Adding and Removing Apps

- **Adding Apps**: To add new apps to your Home Screen, follow these steps:

    o **App Store**: Open the App Store, search for the app you want, then tap *Get* and *Install*. The app icon will automatically appear on your Home Screen.

    o **App Library**: Apps downloaded from the App Store are automatically added to the App Library. Swipe left past your last Home Screen page to access it, then tap and hold an app to add it to the Home Screen.

- **Removing Apps**: If you want to remove apps from the Home Screen:

    o Tap and hold any app icon until all apps start to jiggle.

    o Tap the '-' button on the app you want to delete.

    o Confirm by tapping *Delete*.

2. Creating and Managing Folders

- **Creating Folders**: Organize apps into folders to reduce clutter:

    o Tap and hold an app icon until it starts to jiggle.

    o Drag one app onto another app to create a folder.

    o Enter a name for the folder or use the suggested name.

    o To add more apps, drag them into the folder.

- **Managing Folders**: To manage folders on your Home Screen:

    o Tap and hold a folder to enter editing mode.

○ Rename the folder, rearrange apps within it, or delete the folder by dragging apps out of it.

3. Customizing App Icons with Shortcuts

- **Use Shortcuts**: iOS 18 allows you to customize app icons using Shortcuts for a more personalized look:

  ○ Open the *Shortcuts* app.

  ○ Tap the '+' icon to create a new shortcut.

  ○ Tap *Add Action*, then search for and select *Open App*.

  ○ Choose the app you want to customize, tap *Next*, and then enter a name for your shortcut.

  ○ Tap *Add to Home Screen*, enter the name for your custom icon, and tap *Add*.

  ○ Go to your Home Screen, tap and hold the app icon you want to replace, and select *Edit Home Screen*.

  ○ Tap the app icon's thumbnail, select *Choose Photo*, and pick the image you want to use as the custom icon.

4. Adding and Resizing Widgets

- **Adding Widgets**: Widgets provide quick access to information and actions directly from your Home Screen:

  ○ Tap and hold an empty area on your Home Screen until the apps jiggle.

  ○ Tap the '+' icon in the top-left corner.

  ○ Browse available widgets or use the search bar to find a specific widget.

  ○ Tap on a widget to preview sizes, then tap *Add Widget* to add it to your Home Screen.

Drag the widget to place it where you want, and tap *Done*.

- **Resizing Widgets**: Some widgets can be resized for more customization:

    o Tap and hold the widget you want to resize until it jiggles.

    o Tap *Edit Widget*.

    o Choose the preferred size options available for that widget, then tap *Done*.

5. Changing Wallpaper and Appearance

- **Changing Wallpaper**: Customize your Home Screen background with a new wallpaper:

    o Go to *Settings > Wallpaper > Choose a New Wallpaper*.

    o Select a wallpaper from the options provided, including dynamic, stills, and live wallpapers.

Tap *Set* and choose whether to set it for the Home Screen, Lock Screen, or both.

- **Dynamic Theme Modes**: iOS 18 introduces dynamic themes that adjust based on the time of day and lighting conditions for a more personalized experience:

  o Go to *Settings > Display & Brightness*.

Choose *Light* or *Dark* mode or set it to *Automatic* to switch modes automatically based on ambient light.

6. Organizing and Hiding Pages

- **Organizing Pages**: Arrange your Home Screen pages to prioritize apps and widgets:

  o Tap and hold an empty area on the Home Screen until the apps jiggle.

  o Tap the dots above the Dock to view all Home Screen pages.

  o Drag pages to rearrange them or swipe left on a page and tap *Remove* to delete it (deleted pages can be restored from the App Library).

- **Hiding Pages**: Hide Home Screen pages to streamline your interface:

  o Tap and hold an empty area on the Home Screen until the apps jiggle.

  o Tap the dots above the Dock to view all Home Screen pages.

o   Uncheck the circle under the page you want to hide to remove it from the Home Screen view (hidden pages remain accessible in the App Library).

7. Use App Clips

- **App Clips**: iOS 18 supports App Clips for quick access to specific app features without installing the full app:

    o   When you see an App Clip code or a suggestion banner, tap it to open the App Clip.

    o   Use the App Clip for its specific functionality, such as ordering food or renting a scooter.

    o   App Clips can be added to the Home Screen for easy access and are automatically removed after use.

8. Customizing Control Center

- **Control Center Customization**: Customize the Control Center for quick access to frequently used controls:

    o   Go to *Settings > Control Center*.

    o   Tap *Customize Controls* to add, remove, or reorder controls like Wi-Fi, Bluetooth, screen recording, and more.

Use and Organize Widgets

Widgets in iOS 18 provide quick access to important information and functionalities directly from your Home Screen. They come in various sizes and can be customized to fit your needs and aesthetic preferences:

1. Adding Widgets to Your Home Screen

- **Long Press and Add**:

    o   Tap and hold an empty area on the Home Screen until the apps and widgets start to jiggle.

    o   Tap the '+' icon in the top-left corner of the screen to open the widget gallery.

    o   Browse through the widget categories or use the search bar to find a specific widget.

- Select a widget to see its available sizes (small, medium, large) and preview each size.

- Tap *Add Widget* to place it on your Home Screen.

- Drag the widget to your desired location and tap *Done* to exit jiggle mode.

- **From Existing Widgets**:

  - Swipe right to access the Today View (available from the Home Screen and the Lock Screen).

  - Scroll to the bottom of the Today View and tap *Edit*.

  - Tap the '+' icon in the top-left corner to access the widget gallery.

  - Follow the steps above to add widgets directly to the Today View.

2. Organizing and Arranging Widgets

- **Moving Widgets**:

  - Tap and hold a widget until it starts to jiggle.

  - Drag the widget to your preferred location on the Home Screen.

  - Place widgets adjacent to each other or in gaps between app icons for a cleaner look.

  - Tap *Done* to save your arrangement.

- **Stacking Widgets**:

  - Widget stacks allow you to save space by grouping multiple widgets of the same size:

    - Drag one widget on top of another of the same size to create a stack.

    - Tap the stack to cycle through the widgets.

    - Swipe up or down on the stack to view the next widget.

    - Tap and hold the stack, then choose *Edit Stack* to manage the widgets within it. You can reorder or remove widgets from the stack.

- Use *Smart Stack* for automatically rotating widgets based on your usage patterns, time of day, and other factors.

- **Smart Stack**:
  - o Smart Stack is a special type of widget that automatically rotates widgets based on your activity:
    - Add a Smart Stack from the widget gallery.
    - Tap and hold the stack to edit its contents and preferences.
    - Enable or disable *Smart Rotate* to allow iOS to automatically show the most relevant widget.

3. Customizing Widgets

- **Editing Widgets**:
  - o Some widgets allow for additional customization directly from the Home Screen:
    - Tap and hold a widget until it jiggles, then tap *Edit Widget*.
    - Adjust settings specific to that widget, such as choosing which calendar to display in a Calendar widget or selecting a specific folder for a Photos widget.
    - Tap outside the widget to exit edit mode.

- **Changing Widget Size**:
  - o Widgets come in three sizes: small, medium, and large. You can change the size of a widget to better fit your Home Screen layout:
    - Tap and hold the widget until it jiggles.
    - Tap the '-' button to remove the widget.
    - Tap the '+' icon to add the widget again, selecting a different size this time.

4. Use Widget Recommendations

- **Suggested Widgets**:

- o   iOS 18 can suggest widgets based on your usage and preferences:
    - ▪   Scroll down to the bottom of the widget gallery to find suggested widgets tailored for you.
    - ▪   Add these recommended widgets to your Home Screen for quick access to frequently used apps and services.

- **Proactive Widgets**:
    - o   Some widgets in iOS 18 are proactive and can show relevant information based on your context and activity. For example, the Weather widget might update to show rain alerts or the Calendar widget might highlight your next appointment.

5. Managing Widgets in Today View

- **Adding Widgets to Today View**:
    - o   Swipe right from the Home Screen to access Today View.
    - o   Tap and hold on an empty area or scroll down and tap *Edit*.
    - o   Tap the '+' icon to open the widget gallery and add widgets to Today View.

- **Reordering Widgets in Today View**:
    - o   In Today View, tap and hold a widget until it jiggles.
    - o   Drag the widget up or down to reorder it within Today View.
    - o   Tap *Done* to save your changes.

6. Third-Party Widgets

- **Adding Third-Party Widgets**:
    - o   Many apps now offer their own widgets that you can add to your Home Screen or Today View:
        - ▪   Install the app from the App Store.
        - ▪   Add its widget by following the standard process through the widget gallery.
        - ▪   Customize these widgets as you would with Apple's default widgets.

- **Managing Third-Party Widgets**:

    o   Third-party widgets often come with specific customization options. Tap and hold the widget, then select *Edit Widget* to explore available settings.

    o   Keep apps updated to ensure you have the latest widgets and functionalities.

7. Widget Troubleshooting and Tips

- **Troubleshooting Widgets**:

    o   If a widget isn't updating or displaying correctly:

        ▪   Remove and re-add the widget.

        ▪   Restart your iPhone.

        ▪   Ensure the associated app is up to date.

    o   Check the app's permissions in *Settings* to ensure it has access to the necessary data and services.

- **Widget Tips**:

    o   Use a mix of widgets and app icons to create a balance of information and accessibility.

    o   Group related widgets into stacks to maximize space efficiency.

    o   Experiment with different widget sizes and layouts to find what works best for you.

    o   Keep your most-used widgets at the top of the Home Screen for quick access.

App Library Overview

The App Library, introduced in iOS 14 and refined in iOS 18, provides a new way to organize and access your apps without cluttering your Home Screen. It automatically sorts and categorizes all your apps, making it easier to find and manage them:

1. Accessing the App Library

- **Location**: The App Library is located to the right of your last Home Screen page. To access it, simply swipe left until you reach the App Library.

- **Structure**: The App Library organizes apps into automatically generated categories and provides a search bar at the top for easy navigation.

2. Understanding App Categories

- **Automatically Organized**: The App Library automatically categorizes your apps into folders like Social, Entertainment, Utilities, and Productivity. These categories are based on the app's functionality and how frequently you use them.

- **Folders and Groups**: Each category in the App Library displays the most frequently used apps prominently. Other apps within the same category are grouped into smaller, more compact icons.

  - **Large Icons**: These represent the most used apps in each category and can be launched with a single tap.

  - **Small Icons**: Tapping on the smaller cluster of icons within a category will expand it to show all apps in that category.

3. Use the Search Bar

- **Quick Search**: The search bar at the top of the App Library allows you to quickly find any app by typing its name.

- **Alphabetical List**: When you tap the search bar, the App Library presents an alphabetical list of all your apps, which you can scroll through or use the alphabetical index on the side for quick navigation.

4. Managing Apps in the App Library

- **Adding Apps to the Home Screen**:

  - Tap and hold an app icon in the App Library until a menu appears.

  - Select *Add to Home Screen* to place the app on your Home Screen.

- **Deleting Apps**:

o   Tap and hold an app icon in the App Library.

o   Select *Delete App* from the context menu, then confirm to remove the app from your device.

- **Finding Apps in Folders**:

    o   Tap on a folder to see a full list of apps within that category.

    o   Use this expanded view to find less frequently used apps that might not appear as large icons.

4. **Customizing Home Screen Pages**

The Home Screen can be further customized by arranging apps and widgets in any open space.

Customized Home Screen: iPhone shows the Home Screen with apps and widgets arranged around a photo, and another with a light effect on the Home Screen.

- **Minimizing Clutter**: The App Library helps keep your Home Screen clean by allowing you to move apps off the Home Screen while still keeping them accessible in the App Library.

- **Hiding Home Screen Pages**:

    o Tap and hold on an empty area of the Home Screen until the apps jiggle.

    o Tap the page dots above the Dock to enter the *Edit Pages* view.

    o Uncheck the circles below the pages you want to hide, then tap *Done*.

- **Reorganizing Home Screen Pages**:

    o In the *Edit Pages* view, you can drag pages to reorder them to prioritize certain app layouts.

6. Use App Suggestions and Recently Added

- **App Suggestions**: At the top of the App Library, you'll find a dynamically updated *Suggestions* category that highlights apps you're likely to use next based on your usage patterns.

- **Recently Added**: This category shows your most recently downloaded apps, making it easy to find new additions to your device without searching through all your apps.

7. Moving Apps from the App Library to the Home Screen

App icons can take on a larger appearance for a bold, minimalist look.

iPhone shows app icons with a larger appearance on the Home Screen

- **Drag and Drop**: Tap and hold an app in the App Library until it jiggles, then drag it to the left edge of the screen to place it back on the Home Screen.

- **Add via Context Menu**: Tap and hold an app and select *Add to Home Screen* to move it directly without dragging.

8. Use App Clips from the App Library

- **Accessing App Clips**: App Clips are lightweight versions of apps that allow you to perform specific tasks without downloading the full app. They can be accessed via QR codes, NFC tags, or links.

- **Managing App Clips**:

    o Open the App Library and navigate to the *Recently Added* category to find and manage any recently used App Clips.

o   Tap and hold an App Clip to delete it or view more information.

9. Tips for Efficient Use of the App Library

- Move less frequently used apps to the App Library to keep your Home Screen clean and focused on the apps you use daily.

- Use the search bar and category folders to quickly locate apps instead of scrolling through multiple Home Screen pages.

- Periodically review and reorganize your apps, utilizing the App Library to streamline your Home Screen layout.

10. Exploring Advanced Features

- The App Library uses on-device intelligence to suggest apps based on time, location, and activity, helping you quickly access the apps you need.

- **Enhanced Accessibility**: The alphabetical list and search functions make it easier for users with visual or motor impairments to find and open apps efficiently.

Control Center and Notifications

Access and Customize the Control Center

The Control Center in iOS 18 provides quick access to essential controls and features like Wi-Fi, Bluetooth, brightness, and volume, as well as shortcuts to apps and system functionalities. Customizing it can significantly enhance your iPhone experience by allowing you to tailor it to your needs and preferences:

1. Accessing the Control Center

- **From the Home Screen**: Swipe down from the top-right corner of the screen. This gesture works on all iPhones with Face ID.

- **From the Lock Screen**: Swipe down from the top-right corner of the screen. Make sure Control Center access is enabled on the Lock Screen (Settings > Face ID & Passcode or Touch ID & Passcode > Allow Access When Locked > Control Center).

- **From Within Apps**: Swipe down from the top-right corner while using any app to access the Control Center without exiting the app.

2. Default Controls in the Control Center

The Control Center includes several built-in controls by default:

- **Network Controls**: Includes Airplane Mode, Wi-Fi, Bluetooth, Cellular Data, and AirDrop.

- **Audio Controls**: Access and control media playback and volume.

- **Screen Mirroring**: Quickly mirror your iPhone's display to an Apple TV or AirPlay 2-compatible device.

- **Brightness and Volume Sliders**: Adjust screen brightness and system volume.

- **Flashlight, Timer, Calculator, and Camera**: Shortcuts to commonly used apps and functions.

- **Do Not Disturb**: Toggle the Do Not Disturb mode on and off.

- **Focus Mode**: Access and manage Focus modes for different contexts (Work, Sleep, etc.).

3. Customizing the Control Center

To add, remove, and rearrange controls in the Control Center, follow these steps:

- **Adding Controls**:
  - Open the *Settings* app on your iPhone.
  - Tap *Control Center*.
  - Under the *More Controls* section, find the controls you want to add.
  - Tap the green '+' button next to each control you want to add to the Control Center.
  - Examples of additional controls you can add include:
    - Low Power Mode
    - Screen Recording
    - Notes
    - Magnifier

- QR Code Scanner

- Text Size

- Accessibility Shortcuts

- **Removing Controls**:

  o In the *Control Center* settings, under the *Included Controls* section, find the controls you want to remove.

  o Tap the red '-' button next to each control you want to remove.

  o Tap *Remove* to confirm.

- **Reordering Controls**:

  o In the *Included Controls* section, tap and hold the three horizontal lines next to a control.

  o Drag the control up or down to rearrange its position within the Control Center.

  o The topmost controls appear first in the Control Center.

4. Use Custom Controls

- **Low Power Mode**: Toggle Low Power Mode to extend your iPhone's battery life by reducing background activity and performance.

- **Screen Recording**: Start and stop screen recording with a single tap. The recording will include all on-screen activity and sounds.

- **Notes**: Quickly create a new note or view existing notes directly from the Control Center.

- **Magnifier**: Use your iPhone's camera to magnify objects, useful for reading small text or viewing details.

- **QR Code Scanner**: Instantly scan QR codes to open links, add contacts, or access information without using the camera app.

5. Accessing and Managing Focus Modes

- **Focus Mode**: iOS 18 allows you to manage different Focus modes (like Do Not Disturb, Work, Sleep) from the Control Center:

- o Tap the *Focus* button to switch between different Focus modes or customize settings for each mode.

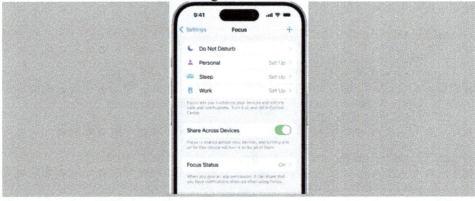

Long press on the *Focus* button to see a detailed menu of available Focus modes and their options.

6. Advanced Control Center Features

- **Haptic Touch and Long Press**: Many controls in the Control Center support additional options via Haptic Touch or a long press:

  - o For example, long pressing the brightness slider reveals Night Shift and True Tone settings.

  - o Long press the network settings cluster to access more detailed Wi-Fi, Bluetooth, and AirDrop options.

- **Dynamic Controls**: Some controls in iOS 18 adapt based on context and usage:

  - o For instance, the media playback control shows the currently playing track or video.

  - o AirPlay controls will dynamically display available devices when connected to external displays or speakers.

7. Use Control Center with Accessibility Features

- **Accessibility Shortcuts**: Customize the Control Center to include shortcuts to accessibility features such as VoiceOver, Magnifier, or AssistiveTouch:

- Go to *Settings* > *Accessibility* > *Accessibility Shortcut* and select the desired options.

- Add the *Accessibility Shortcuts* control to the Control Center for quick access.

- **Hearing and Vision Controls**: Include controls for hearing aids, sound recognition, and display accommodations to the Control Center for easier access.

8. Control Center Tips and Tricks

- **Quick Adjustments**: Use the Control Center to quickly adjust settings without navigating through the Settings app.

- **Access Anywhere**: Enable Control Center access from apps and the Lock Screen to quickly toggle settings or access shortcuts.

- **Customize Regularly**: Periodically review and update your Control Center layout to keep it aligned with your changing needs and frequently used features.

9. Troubleshooting Control Center Issues

- **Access Problems**: If you can't access the Control Center:

  - Check-in *Settings* > *Control Center* that access is enabled on the Lock Screen and within apps.

  - Restart your iPhone if the issue persists.

- **Unresponsive Controls**: If certain controls aren't responding:

  - Make sure the associated feature or app is installed and up-to-date.

  - Restart your iPhone or reset network settings if network-related controls are unresponsive.

Manage Notifications

Notifications are a crucial part of staying informed and connected on your iPhone. iOS 18 brings enhanced features to manage, customize, and prioritize your notifications. This ensures you only see what's important to you:

1. Accessing Notification Settings

- **Settings App**:

  - o Open the *Settings* app on your iPhone.

  - o Tap *Notifications* to access the main notification settings page.

  - o Here, you can configure general notification settings and individual app notifications.

- **Quick Settings**:

  - o Swipe down from the top centre or top-left corner of the screen to open the Notification Center.

  - o Swipe left on a notification and tap *Options* to access quick settings for that app.

  - o Alternatively, swipe left and tap *Manage* for more detailed settings options.

2. Configuring Notification Style and Delivery

- **Banner Style**:

  - o Go to *Settings* > *Notifications* > [App Name].

  - o Choose between *Temporary* (banners that disappear automatically) and *Persistent* (banners that remain until you dismiss them) for the style of banner notifications.

- **Notification Previews**:

- Decide when notification previews appear: *Always*, *When Unlocked*, or *Never*.

- Go to *Settings > Notifications > Show Previews* and choose your preference. This affects all apps by default.

- **Grouping Notifications**:

  - iOS 18 can group notifications by app or automatically based on context.

  - Go to *Settings > Notifications >* [App Name] *> Notification Grouping*.

  - Select *Automatic* (intelligently grouped by app), *By App* (grouped by app), or *Off* (no grouping).

- **Scheduling Notifications**:

  - Use *Notification Summary* to schedule non-urgent notifications to be delivered at specific times.

  - Go to *Settings > Notifications > Scheduled Summary*.

  - Turn on *Scheduled Summary* and select apps whose notifications you want to include.

  - Choose delivery times for your summaries, such as morning and evening updates.

3. Managing Notification Behavior for Individual Apps

- **Allow Notifications**:

  - Go to *Settings > Notifications >* [App Name].

  - Toggle *Allow Notifications* on or off to enable or disable notifications for that app.

- **Alert Style and Sounds**:
  - Choose how alerts are delivered: *Lock Screen*, *Notification Center*, and/or *Banners*.
  - Customize alert sounds and vibration patterns under the *Sounds* section for each app.

- **Critical Alerts**:
  - Some apps can send critical alerts that bypass Do Not Disturb and mute settings.
  - Critical alerts are used for urgent notifications, like health or security alerts.
  - Manage these in the app's specific notification settings.

4. Use Focus Modes with Notifications

- **Focus Mode Integration**:
  - Focus modes allow you to filter notifications based on your current activity (e.g., Work, Sleep).
  - Go to *Settings > Focus* and select a Focus mode to configure it.
  - Under the *Allowed Notifications* section, choose which people and apps can notify you during this mode.

- **Customizing Focus Modes**:
    - Customize each Focus mode's settings to allow notifications from specific contacts and apps.
    - You can also enable *Time Sensitive Notifications* to ensure critical messages are delivered even during a Focus session.

5. Managing Notification Center

- **Viewing Notifications**:
    - Swipe down from the top centre or top-left corner of the screen to access the Notification Center.
    - Notifications are grouped by app and time, showing recent alerts at the top.

- **Clearing Notifications**:
    - Clear individual notifications by swiping left and tapping *Clear*.
    - Clear all notifications from a specific app by tapping the 'X' next to the app name and then tapping *Clear*.
    - To clear all notifications, scroll to the top of the Notification Center tap and hold the 'X', then tap *Clear All Notifications*.

6. Use Notification Interactions

- **Interactive Notifications**:
    - Many notifications support direct interactions without opening the app.

- Swipe down on a notification to expand it and reveal quick actions, like replying to messages or viewing more details.

- Long press or Haptic Touch on a notification to access additional options and actions.

- **Notification Actions**:

  - Different notifications offer various actions, such as *Mark as Read*, *Reply*, or *Delete*.

  - Custom actions specific to apps, like *Archive* for emails or *Like* for social media notifications, can also be available.

7. Managing Notification Badges

- **App Icon Badges**:

  - Badges are the red notification dots that appear on app icons indicating unread notifications.

  - To manage badges, go to *Settings > Notifications > [App Name] >* toggle *Badges* on or off.

- **Clearing Badges**:

  - Open the app to clear the badge count or manage settings within the app if it offers controls for badge notifications.

8. Use Do Not Disturb and Notification Mute Options

- **Do Not Disturb**:

  - Enable Do Not Disturb to silence all notifications.

  - Go to *Settings > Focus > Do Not Disturb* to schedule Do Not Disturb or customize allowed notifications.

  - Quickly enable Do Not Disturb from the Control Center by tapping the crescent moon icon.

- **Muting Notifications**:

  - Mute specific app notifications directly from the Notification Center by swiping left on a notification and tapping *Options > Mute for 1 Hour* or *Mute for Today*.

o Manage persistent mute settings in *Settings* > *Notifications* > [App Name] > toggle *Allow Notifications* off.

9. Notification Privacy and Security

- **Notification Privacy**:

    o Adjust notification privacy settings to control what information is displayed on the Lock Screen.

    o Go to *Settings* > *Notifications* > *Show Previews* and choose *When Unlocked* or *Never* for more privacy.

- **Secure Notifications**:

    o Sensitive information can be protected by enabling *Show Previews* only *When Unlocked*.

    o Ensure that apps with sensitive data are set to deliver notifications with minimal information on the Lock Screen.

10. Notification Troubleshooting and Tips

- **Notification Delivery Issues**:

    o If notifications aren't appearing, check the app's notification settings and ensure *Allow Notifications* is enabled.

    o Make sure *Do Not Disturb* or Focus modes aren't silencing notifications unintentionally.

    o Restart your iPhone and update apps to resolve any glitches.

- **Optimizing Notifications**:

    o Regularly review and update your notification settings to avoid clutter and ensure you're only receiving important alerts.

    o Use the *Scheduled Summary* to consolidate less urgent notifications and reduce distraction.

Notification Summary and Scheduling

iOS 18 introduces advanced notification management features to help you control how and when you receive alerts. The *Notification Summary* and scheduling tools enable you to consolidate non-urgent notifications and deliver them at specific times, reducing distractions and keeping your Notification Center tidy:

1. Understanding Notification Summary

- Notification Summary collects and organizes non-urgent notifications from your apps and delivers them in scheduled summaries at times you choose. This feature helps you stay focused by reducing interruptions and providing a concise overview of your notifications.

- **Functionality**: You can schedule multiple summaries throughout the day, ensuring you receive updates when it's convenient for you rather than immediately.

2. Setting Up Notification Summary

- **Accessing Settings**:
  - o Open the *Settings* app on your iPhone.
  - o Tap *Notifications*.
  - o Select *Scheduled Summary*.

- **Enabling Scheduled Summary**:
  - o Toggle *Scheduled Summary* to the on position.
  - o If prompted, follow the on-screen instructions to enable the feature.

- **Choosing Apps for Summary**:
  - o In the *App Summary* section, you'll see a list of all your apps.
  - o Toggle on the apps you want to include in your scheduled summary. Notifications from these apps will appear in your summaries instead of immediately.

3. Configuring Summary Schedule

- **Setting Delivery Times**:
  - o After enabling *Scheduled Summary*, tap *Set Up Summary*.
  - o You can add multiple times for receiving summaries. For example, you might want one in the morning, one in the afternoon, and one in the evening.

o   Tap *Add Summary* to set additional delivery times.

- **Adjusting Summary Order**:

  o   To change the order of summaries, tap *Edit* next to the existing delivery times.

  o   Drag and drop to rearrange the order of the summaries.

  o   Tap *Done* to save your changes.

4. Managing Notification Summary Content

- **Prioritizing Apps**:

  o   In the *App Summary* settings, apps are listed with a frequency indicator showing how many notifications they send daily.

  o   Use this information to prioritize which apps should be in your summaries, focusing on those that send frequent but non-urgent notifications.

- **Editing App Inclusion**:

  o   Return to the *App Summary* section anytime to add or remove apps from the summary.

  o   Toggle off any app you no longer want to include in the scheduled summaries.

5. Viewing and Interacting with Summaries

- **Accessing Summaries**:

  o   Scheduled summaries appear in the Notification Center at the times you've set.

  o   To view a summary, swipe down from the top centre or top-left corner of the screen to open the Notification Center.

  o   Summaries are clearly labelled and contain grouped notifications from the apps you've selected.

- **Interacting with Notifications**:

  o   Tap on a notification within the summary to open it and see more details.

- o Use quick actions (like replying to a message or marking an email as read) directly from the summary, just as you would with individual notifications.

6. Use Focus Mode with Notification Summary

- **Combining Focus Modes**:
  - o Use Focus modes to manage when and how you receive notifications outside your scheduled summaries.
  - o Go to *Settings > Focus* and select or create a Focus mode.
  - o Under *Allowed Notifications*, you can customize which apps and contacts can send you notifications while the Focus mode is active.

- **Enhanced Control**:
  - o Focus modes can automatically adjust based on time, location, or app usage, providing a dynamic approach to managing notifications alongside your scheduled summaries.

7. Advanced Scheduling and Customization

- **Time-Sensitive Notifications**:
  - o Certain important notifications, like calendar events or reminders, can bypass the summary and be delivered immediately.
  - o Go to *Settings > Notifications > [App Name]* and toggle on *Time Sensitive Notifications* if you want these alerts to bypass summaries and Focus modes.

- **Personalized Summary Settings**:
  - o In *Scheduled Summary* settings, you can tailor how summaries are displayed and managed.
  - o Choose between *Stack* or *List* views for how notifications appear within summaries.
  - o Enable or disable *Notification Grouping* within summaries for more organized viewing.

8. Tips for Effective Notification Management

- **Regular Review**:

    o Periodically review which apps are included in your summary and adjust as needed based on your changing usage and preferences.

    o Keep the number of included apps manageable to ensure summaries remain concise and useful.

- **Strategic Scheduling**:

    o Set your summary delivery times to align with your daily routine, such as during breaks or at the start and end of your workday.

    o Avoid scheduling summaries during times when you need to focus or when you are less likely to check your phone.

9. Troubleshooting Notification Summary Issues

- **Missing Notifications**:

    o If you're missing important notifications, check that the app is not included in the summary or is marked as time-sensitive.

    o Ensure that the scheduled summary times are set correctly and that you're checking the Notification Center during those times.

- **Excessive Notifications**:

    o If summaries are becoming too cluttered, reduce the number of included apps or adjust the frequency of summary deliveries.

    o Consider disabling notifications for less important apps or using Focus modes to manage immediate notifications.

Gestures and Multitasking

Essential Gestures for Navigation

Navigating your iPhone has never been more intuitive and efficient, thanks to a wide range of touch gestures that make interacting with iOS 18 seamless and enjoyable. This guide will cover the essential gestures you need to master:

1. Basic Navigation Gestures

- **Swipe Up**:

  - **Home Gesture**: Swipe up from the bottom edge of the screen to return to the Home Screen from any app.

  - **App Switcher**: Swipe up from the bottom and pause in the middle of the screen to access the App Switcher, showing all open apps for quick switching or closing.

  - **Control Center**: On iPhones with a notch, swipe down from the top-right corner to open the Control Center. On iPhones with a Home button, swipe up from the bottom for the Control Center.

- **Swipe Down**:

  - **Notification Center**: Swipe down from the top-centre or top-left corner to access the Notification Center, where you can view and manage notifications.

  - **Search**: Swipe down on the Home Screen to access the Spotlight search, where you can search for apps, contacts, files, and web results quickly.

- **Tap**:

  - **Single Tap**: Tap once on an app icon to open it, or on any button to activate it.

  - **Double Tap**: Double-tap for actions like zooming in on photos or webpages, or to perform quick tasks in supported apps.

2. Advanced Navigation Gestures

- **Swipe Left or Right**:

  - **App Switching**: Swipe left or right along the bottom edge of the screen to quickly switch between recently used apps.

  - **Delete Actions**: Swipe left on notifications, messages, or emails to reveal delete or archive options.

- **Pinch and Spread**:

  - **Zoom In and Out**: Pinch two fingers together to zoom out or spread them apart to zoom in on photos, maps, and other content.

- o **App Icons**: Pinch on the Home Screen to access the layout customization options like adding widgets or adjusting the app grid.

- **Long Press (Haptic Touch)**:

  - o **Contextual Menus**: Press and hold on to app icons or notifications to access quick actions or additional options.

  - o **Rearrange Apps**: Long press on any app icon until the icons start jiggling to rearrange or delete apps.

3. Gestures for Multitasking

- **Split View and Slide Over** (iPads only, applicable when using iPhones with larger screens or when connected to external monitors):

  - o **Split View**: Drag an app from the Dock to the left or right edge of the screen to use two apps side by side.

  - o **Slide Over**: Drag an app from the Dock to the centre of the screen to use it in a floating window above another app.

- **Quick Notes**:

  - o **Swipe Up and Tap**: Swipe up from the bottom right corner to access Quick Notes, allowing you to jot down notes from anywhere in the OS.

4. Gestures for Accessibility

- **Reachability**:

  - o **Swipe Down**: Swipe down on the bottom edge of the screen (near the centre or bottom-left corner) to bring the top of the screen within easy reach.

  - o **Double Tap Home Button**: On iPhones with a Home button, lightly double tap the Home button to activate Reachability.

- **AssistiveTouch**:

  - o **Custom Gestures**: Enable AssistiveTouch from *Settings > Accessibility > Touch > AssistiveTouch*. This provides a floating on-screen button for custom gestures and shortcuts.

5. Gestures for Interacting with Notifications and Widgets

- **Manage Notifications**:

    o **Swipe Left on Notifications**: Swipe left on a notification in the Notification Center to reveal options for managing or clearing it.

    o **Swipe Down on Widgets**: Swipe down from the top of a widget stack to reveal more detailed information or additional widgets.

- **Widget Interactions**:

    o **Long Press**: Long press on a widget to edit it, remove it, or interact with its available options.

    o **Swipe Between Widgets**: If you have a stack of widgets, swipe up or down to switch between them.

6. Gestures for Text Editing

- **Cursor Control**:

    o **Tap and Hold**: Tap and hold on text to bring up the magnifying glass for precise cursor placement.

    o **Drag to Select**: Tap and drag over text to select it quickly for editing or copying.

- **Quick Actions**:

    o **Three-Finger Swipe**: Swipe left with three fingers to undo, and swipe right to redo.

    o **Pinch In/Out with Three Fingers**: Pinch in with three fingers to copy, pinch out with three fingers to paste.

7. Gestures for Photos and Media

A simplified, single view displays a familiar grid and helpful new collections.

Collections give users a way to browse by themes, like recent days or trips, without having to organize content into albums.

iPhone shows a photo grid and collections in the Photos app, and another collection labelled Recent Days and People & Pets in the Photos app.

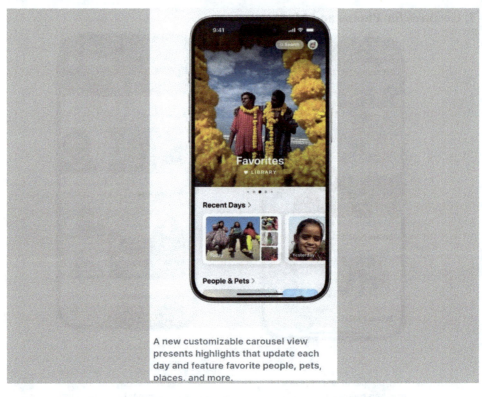

A new customizable carousel view presents highlights that update each day and feature favorite people, pets, places, and more.

- **Photo Navigation**:

    ○ **Swipe Left or Right**: Swipe left or right to move between photos in the Photos app.

    ○ **Zoom and Pan**: Use pinch to zoom and drag to pan around a photo.

- **Media Controls**:

    ○ **Tap to Play/Pause**: Tap on the screen when viewing a video or playing music to reveal and control playback options.

    ○ **Drag to Seek**: Drag the playback bar to fast forward or rewind in videos and music tracks.

8. Gestures for Safari and Web Browsing

- **Tab Management**:

o **Swipe Left or Right**: Swipe left or right on the address bar to switch between open tabs.

o **Pinch Close**: Pinch closed on the tab view screen to return to the tab switcher.

- **Navigation**:

o **Swipe from Edge**: Swipe from the left edge of the screen to go back to the previous page, and swipe from the right edge to go forward.

Use Multitasking Features

iOS 18 enhances your ability to multitask with powerful features that allow you to use multiple apps simultaneously, switch between tasks efficiently, and stay productive on the go:

1. App Switcher

- **Accessing the App Switcher**:

o **Swipe Up and Hold**: Swipe up from the bottom edge of the screen and pause briefly in the centre to reveal the App Switcher, displaying all currently open apps.

o **Double Press Home Button**: On iPhones with a Home button, double press the Home button to open the App Switcher.

- **Navigating the App Switcher**:

o **Swipe Left or Right**: Swipe left or right to browse through open apps.

o **Tap to Switch**: Tap on any app card to switch to that app instantly.

o **Swipe Up to Close**: Swipe up on an app card to close the app and remove it from the switcher.

2. Quick App Switching

- **Swiping Between Apps**:

o **Swipe Left or Right**: On the bottom edge of the screen, swipe left or right to quickly switch between the most recently used apps.

- **App Handoff**:

    - o **Continuity**: With Handoff, you can start a task on one Apple device and pick it up on another. For example, start composing an email on your iPhone and finish it on your iPad or Mac.

    - o **Use Handoff**: Ensure both devices are signed into the same iCloud account, and enable Handoff in *Settings > General > AirPlay & Handoff*. Then, apps that support Handoff will show a small icon on the Dock or App Switcher.

3. Picture-in-Picture (PiP)

- **Enabling Picture-in-Picture**:

    - o **Starting PiP**: When watching a video or during a FaceTime call, swipe up or press the Home button to start Picture-in-Picture mode. The video will shrink to a floating window that can be moved around the screen.

    - o **PiP Controls**: Use the on-screen controls to play/pause or close the PiP window. You can resize the window by pinching or expand it back to full screen by tapping the PiP icon.

- **Use PiP with Other Apps**:

    - o **Multitasking with PiP**: Continue using other apps while the PiP window remains on the screen. You can drag the PiP window to any corner of the screen for convenience.

    - o **Hiding PiP**: Temporarily move the PiP window off the edge of the screen by dragging it to one side. It will reappear when needed.

4. Slide Over and Split View (iPads only, relevant for larger iPhones)

While these features are primarily designed for iPads, they offer a glimpse of multitasking potential that influences how larger iPhones or iOS with external displays handle multitasking.

- **Slide Over**:

    - o **Launching Slide Over** Drag an app from the Dock or Home Screen and drop it on the screen to open it in Slide Over mode, floating above the main app.

- ○ **Switching Slide Over Apps**: Swipe left or right on the Slide Over bar at the bottom to switch between multiple apps in Slide Over.

- ○ **Moving Slide Over Window**: Drag the top handle of the Slide Over window to move it to the left or right side of the screen.

- **Split View**:

  - ○ **Launching Split View**: Drag an app from the Dock or Home Screen and drop it to the left or right side of the screen to open it in Split View alongside another app.

  - ○ **Adjusting Split View**: Use the divider between the apps to resize them. Drag the divider to the edge of the screen to return to full screen for one app.

5. Quick Notes

- **Accessing Quick Notes**:

  - ○ **From Control Center**: Add Quick Notes to the Control Center for easy access. Go to *Settings* > *Control Center* > *Customize Controls* and add Quick Notes.

  - ○ **Use Gestures**: Swipe up from the bottom right corner to bring up Quick Notes, allowing you to jot down notes from any screen.

- **Use Quick Notes**:

  - ○ **Creating Notes**: Use the Quick Note interface to write down ideas, lists, or reminders quickly.

  - ○ **Linking Notes**: Quick Notes can link to content within apps, such as Safari pages or email messages, for easy reference.

6. Drag and Drop

- **Use Drag and Drop**:

  - ○ **Selecting Items**: Tap and hold on a text, image, or file until it lifts slightly, indicating it's ready to be dragged.

  - ○ **Dragging Across Apps**: Use another finger to navigate to a different app and drop the item where you want it (e.g., dragging a photo from Photos into a message in Messages).

- **Multitasking with Drag and Drop**:

  - ○ **Dragging Multiple Items**: Select multiple items by tapping additional ones while holding the first, then drag them all at once.

  - ○ **Cross-App Functionality**: Move text, links, images, or files between apps that support drag and drop, enhancing productivity and seamless multitasking.

7. Siri and Voice Control

- **Use Siri for Multitasking**:

  - ○ **Voice Commands**: Activate Siri by holding the Side button or saying "Hey Siri" and use voice commands to open apps, set reminders, or perform tasks while you continue using another app.

  - ○ **Voice Control**: Enable Voice Control from *Settings > Accessibility > Voice Control* to navigate and interact with your device using voice commands without touching the screen.

- **Hands-Free Multitasking**:

  - ○ **Dictation**: Use dictation to input text in any text field, allowing you to type while multitasking hands-free.

Switching Between Apps

Whether you're quickly jumping between recently used apps or managing multiple tasks at once, these features are designed to keep you productive and in control. Here's how to make the most of app switching on your iPhone.

1. Use the App Switcher

The App Switcher is a core feature for managing and switching between open apps efficiently.

- **Accessing the App Switcher**:

  - ○ **Gesture-Based Navigation**: Swipe up from the bottom edge of the screen and pause in the middle to bring up the App Switcher.

  - ○ **Home Button Navigation**: Double press the Home button to access the App Switcher (for devices with a Home button).

- **Navigating the App Switcher**:

o **Swipe Left or Right**: Swipe horizontally to browse through open apps.

o **Tap to Switch**: Tap on any app card to switch to that app instantly.

o **Swipe Up to Close Apps**: Swipe up on an app card to close the app and remove it from the switcher.

2. Quick App Switching Gestures

For rapid switching between recent apps, iOS 18 offers several quick gestures.

- **Swiping Between Recent Apps**:

    o **Swipe Left or Right**: Swipe left or right along the bottom edge of the screen to cycle through your most recently used apps. This gesture allows you to quickly return to a previous app without opening the App Switcher.

- **Use Home Bar Gestures**:

    o **Swipe Up and Pause**: Swipe up and hold to view all open apps in the App Switcher.

    o **Swipe Across**: Swipe across the Home bar to quickly switch back and forth between apps.

3. Use the Dock on iPad (and larger iPhones with external displays)

While primarily an iPad feature, understanding how the Dock works can enhance multitasking knowledge, especially with iPhones connected to larger displays or with the Universal Control feature.

- **Accessing the Dock**:

    o **From the Home Screen**: The Dock is always visible at the bottom of the Home Screen.

    o **From Within an App**: Swipe up slightly from the bottom of the screen to reveal the Dock while inside an app.

- **Switching Apps Using the Dock**:

    o **Tap an App in the Dock**: Simply tap an app icon in the Dock to open it. This is especially useful for frequently used apps.

o **Drag and Drop for Multitasking**: Drag an app from the Dock to the left or right side of the screen to open it in Split View or Slide Over mode (primarily on iPads but also applicable in larger screen or dual-screen settings).

4. Picture-in-Picture (PiP) Mode

Picture-in-Picture allows you to continue using one app while a video or FaceTime call plays in a small, resizable window.

- **Enabling PiP Mode**:

  o **Use the Home Gesture**: While watching a video or during a FaceTime call, swipe up from the bottom or press the Home button to activate PiP mode. The video will shrink into a floating window.

  o **Use Controls**: Some apps have a PiP button directly within their playback controls.

- **Managing PiP Windows**:

  o **Move the PiP Window**: Drag the PiP window to any corner of the screen for convenience.

  o **Resize the PiP Window**: Pinch to zoom to resize the PiP window.

  o **Hide and Reveal PiP**: Drag the PiP window off the screen edge to hide it temporarily. Tap the edge to bring it back.

5. Universal Control and Continuity

Universal Control and Continuity features allow seamless transitions between Apple devices.

- **Use Universal Control**:

  o **Seamless Control**: Move your cursor or perform gestures across multiple Apple devices with a single set of inputs. For example, start a task on your Mac and continue it on your iPhone without interruption.

  o **Drag and Drop Across Devices**: Drag files or content from your iPhone to an iPad or Mac using Universal Control.

- **Use Continuity**:

- o **Handoff Between Devices**: Start an activity on one device (e.g., browsing Safari on your iPhone) and continue on another (e.g., your iPad or Mac) seamlessly.

- o **AirDrop for Fast Switching**: Quickly share files, photos, or documents between devices to switch tasks without hassle.

6. Split View and Slide Over (iPads and large screens)

While mainly for iPads, understanding Split View and Slide Over can provide insights into multitasking in environments where your iPhone is part of a larger ecosystem, such as when using an external display.

- **Use Split View**:

  - o **Open Two Apps Side by Side**: Drag an app from the Dock to the left or right edge to enter Split View.

  - o **Resize Split View**: Adjust the divider to change how much space each app takes up.

- **Use Slide Over**:

  - o **Floating Window**: Drag an app from the Dock to the center of the screen to open it in Slide Over mode.

  - o **Switching Slide Over Apps**: Swipe left or right on the Slide Over bar at the bottom to switch between apps in Slide Over.

7. Use Quick Notes for Fast Access

Quick Notes allows you to quickly jot down notes while multitasking.

- **Accessing Quick Notes**:

  - o **From Control Center**: Add Quick Notes to your Control Center for easy access. Go to *Settings > Control Center* and add *Quick Notes*.

  - o **Gesture Access**: Swipe up from the bottom-right corner to bring up Quick Notes from anywhere in the OS.

- **Linking and Managing Quick Notes**:

  - o **Creating Contextual Notes**: Quick Notes can link directly to content within apps like Safari or Mail, making it easy to reference while multitasking.

o **Managing Notes**: Access your Quick Notes in the Notes app for full editing and organization.

Spotlight and Siri

Use Spotlight Search

Spotlight Search is a powerful feature in iOS 18 that allows you to quickly find and access apps, contacts, documents, and more directly from your Home Screen. It integrates with Siri Suggestions and supports advanced search capabilities, making it an essential tool for navigating and managing your iPhone:

1. Accessing Spotlight Search

- **From the Home Screen**:

  o **Swipe Down**: Simply swipe down on any part of the Home Screen (not the top edge) to reveal the Spotlight Search bar at the top of the screen.

  o **Use the Search Bar**: Tap on the search bar to activate it and bring up the keyboard for typing your query.

- **From the App Library**:

  o **Swipe to App Library**: Swipe left to the last page of the Home Screen to open the App Library.

  o **Search in App Library**: Use the search bar at the top of the App Library to find apps quickly.

- **From the Lock Screen**:

  o **Swipe Down**: On the Lock Screen, swipe down to access the Spotlight Search directly without unlocking your device.

2. Performing Searches

- **Basic Searches**:

  o **Type Queries**: Begin typing your query in the search bar. Spotlight will dynamically update search results as you type.

  o **Voice Search**: Tap the microphone icon to dictate your search query if you prefer using voice input.

- **Search Categories**:

  - **Apps and Contacts**: Quickly find and launch apps or contact individuals by typing their name or related keywords.

  - **Messages and Emails**: Search through your messages and emails by entering specific keywords or contact names.

  - **Web and Maps**: Perform web searches or find locations directly from Spotlight. Results include web links and map directions.

  - **Files and Documents**: Locate documents, notes, or files stored on your device or in iCloud.

  - **Settings and Shortcuts**: Access system settings or shortcuts to specific functions within apps.

- **Advanced Searches**:

  - **Use Natural Language**: Enter queries in natural language, such as "photos from last week" or "emails from John."

  - **Spotlight's AI Suggestions**: Take advantage of Siri's proactive suggestions based on your usage patterns and frequent actions.

3. Use Siri Suggestions

- **Proactive Suggestions**:

- o **Quick Access**: As you begin typing, Spotlight provides proactive Siri Suggestions based on your usage patterns, such as recent contacts, apps, or frequently accessed files.

- o **Actionable Items**: Siri Suggestions can include actions like calling a contact, opening an app, or accessing a specific setting.

- **Siri Knowledge**:

  - o **Contextual Information**: Siri can also provide information related to your query, such as sports scores, weather updates, or news.

  - o **Search Integration**: Suggested search results from Siri Knowledge can link to web content, maps, or other apps.

4. Managing Search Results

- **Refining Searches**:

  - o **Filter Results**: Use specific keywords or phrases to narrow down search results.

  - o **Scroll Through Results**: Scroll down to see more categories and expanded results as Spotlight organizes content into apps, files, web results, and more.

- **Interacting with Results**:

  - o **Tap to Open**: Tap on a search result to open the corresponding app, contact, file, or web page directly.

  - o **Long Press Options**: Long press on a search result to reveal additional actions, such as quick calls, messages, or context menus.

  - o **Preview and Share**: For certain items like emails, documents, or contacts, you can preview or share directly from Spotlight without opening the full app.

5. Customizing Spotlight Search

- **Search Settings**:

  - o **Manage Searchable Content**: Go to *Settings > Siri & Search* to customize what content appears in Spotlight searches. You can enable or disable specific apps or categories.

- o **Control Suggestions**: Adjust Siri Suggestions and other search preferences in *Settings > Siri & Search > Suggestions*.

- o **Privacy Controls**: Spotlight respects your privacy settings, only indexing and suggesting content based on your preferences and data access permissions.

- **App Integration**:

  - o **Enable App Content**: Allow apps to show their content in Spotlight searches by enabling them in the search settings.

  - o **Spotlight Actions**: Some apps offer specific actions or deep links that appear directly in search results, providing shortcuts to tasks like sending messages or starting a navigation.

6. Use Spotlight Search with Siri and Shortcuts

- **Voice Integration**:

  - o **Ask Siri**: Use Siri to perform searches by voice, such as "Search for photos from last year" or "Find emails from Mary."

  - o **Siri Shortcuts**: Integrate your favourite Spotlight searches into Siri Shortcuts for quick access via voice commands or shortcuts.

- **Creating Custom Shortcuts**:

  - o **Add to Shortcuts**: Save frequent Spotlight search queries as custom shortcuts for one-tap access.

  - o **Automate with Shortcuts**: Use the Shortcuts app to create automated workflows that include Spotlight searches or actions based on search results.

Enhancements to Siri and Voice Commands in iOS 18

With the significant enhancement to Siri and Apple's intelligent voice assistant, iOS 18 may have expanded your device's capabilities with new features and improvements. From more natural interactions to deeper integration with apps and services, here's how Siri and voice commands have evolved in iOS 18:

iPhone indicates the user type to Siri.

1. Natural Language Understanding

- **Improved Conversational Skills**:
  - Siri in iOS 18 has enhanced natural language processing capabilities, allowing it to better understand context and complex queries.
  - It can handle more nuanced commands and questions, making interactions with Siri feel more natural and responsive.

2. Proactive Siri Suggestions

- **Predictive Intelligence**:
  - Siri now offers proactive suggestions based on your usage patterns, location, time of day, and app interactions.
  - It can suggest actions, reminders, and information relevant to your routine, helping you stay organized and efficient.

3. Enhanced Voice Recognition

- **Personalized Voice Recognition**:
  - Siri can recognize and respond to different voices, providing personalized responses and content based on individual user profiles.
  - This feature enhances privacy and customization by tailoring Siri's responses and suggestions to specific users.

4. Expanded Integration with Apps and Services

- **App Actions via Siri**:
  - Siri can execute tasks within third-party apps using voice commands, such as sending messages, ordering food, or controlling smart home devices.
  - Developers can integrate Siri shortcuts into their apps, allowing users to create custom voice commands for specific app actions.

5. Improved Accessibility Features

- **Voice Control**:
  - iOS 18 enhances Voice Control capabilities, allowing users to navigate and interact with their devices entirely hands-free.
  - This feature is particularly useful for users with mobility impairments, enabling them to perform tasks like opening apps, composing messages, or browsing the web using voice commands.

6. Multilingual Support

- **Expanded Language Support**:
  - Siri in iOS 18 supports a broader range of languages and dialects, improving accessibility and usability for users worldwide.
  - Users can interact with Siri in their preferred language, enhancing the assistant's global appeal and functionality.

7. Smart Home Integration

- **HomeKit Commands**:

- o Siri's integration with HomeKit devices allows users to control smart home accessories using voice commands.

  - o You can adjust lighting, temperature, and security settings hands-free, making home automation more convenient and accessible.

8. Privacy and Security

- **On-Device Processing**:

  - o Siri in iOS 18 performs more tasks locally on the device, enhancing privacy by reducing the need for data to be sent to Apple servers.

  - o Voice recognition and personalization features are designed to protect user data and ensure secure interactions with Siri.

9. Siri Shortcuts

- **Customizable Shortcuts**:

  - o iOS 18 expands Siri Shortcuts with more options for creating custom commands that link multiple actions across different apps.

  - o Users can set up personalized workflows and automate tasks with a single voice command or tap.

10. Interactive Siri Responses

- **Visual and Contextual Responses**:

  - o Siri can provide more interactive responses with visual elements on the screen, such as displaying information cards or images related to your query.

  - o Contextual awareness allows Siri to follow up on previous questions or actions, providing a more cohesive user experience.

Siri Shortcuts and Automation

Siri Shortcuts and automation features in iOS 18 empower users to streamline tasks, automate workflows, and enhance productivity by creating personalized shortcuts for frequently performed actions. These tools leverage Siri's intelligence to anticipate user needs and execute complex tasks with a single voice command or tap:

1. Introduction to Siri Shortcuts

- **Definition**:

  - **Custom Commands**: Siri Shortcuts allow users to create custom voice commands or shortcuts to perform specific actions across apps and services.

  - **Personalized Automation**: Automate tasks by chaining together actions that can be triggered by a voice command, tap, or scheduled event.

- **Accessing Siri Shortcuts**:

  - **Shortcuts App**: Use the Shortcuts app pre-installed on iOS 18 to create, manage, and discover shortcuts.

  - **Siri Suggestions**: Siri learns from your routine and suggests relevant shortcuts on the lock screen, search, and Siri suggestions widget.

2. Creating Siri Shortcuts

- **Building Shortcuts**:

  - **Shortcut Editor**: Use the intuitive interface of the Shortcuts app to create custom shortcuts by combining multiple steps and actions.

  - **Actions Library**: Browse a vast library of actions supported by apps and services to add to your shortcuts.

- **Examples**:

  - **Routine Tasks**: Create a shortcut to send a message to a specific contact, play a favourite playlist, and turn on smart home lights with a single command.

  - **Workflow Automation**: Chain together actions like sending a daily summary email, checking the weather, and setting reminders in one shortcut.

3. Use Siri Shortcuts

- **Activation Methods**:

- o **Voice Commands**: Trigger shortcuts using voice commands prefixed with "Hey Siri," followed by your custom phrase.

- o **Widgets and App**: Access shortcuts from the Shortcuts widget on the Home Screen or within the Shortcuts app itself.

- o **Lock Screen and Siri Suggestions**: Siri suggests relevant shortcuts based on your usage patterns and current context, making them easily accessible.

- **Examples**:

  - o **Hands-Free Operations**: Initiate hands-free calls, compose messages, or start navigation directions using personalized shortcuts.

  - o **Contextual Shortcuts**: Automate tasks based on location, time of day, or specific events to enhance efficiency.

4. Automation with Shortcuts

- **Scheduled Automation**:

  - o **Time-Based Triggers**: Set up shortcuts to execute actions at specific times or intervals, such as turning on lights at sunset or receiving a morning briefing.

  - o **Location-Based Triggers**: Automate actions when arriving or leaving specific locations, such as adjusting home thermostat settings.

- **Examples**:

  - o **Morning Routine**: Automatically play a morning playlist, read news headlines, and provide commute updates when your alarm goes off.

  - o **Workplace Settings**: Adjust device settings, launch meeting preparation shortcuts, and send status updates based on your calendar events.

5. Advanced Shortcuts Features

- **Conditional Logic**:

- o **If-Else Actions**: Integrate conditional statements into shortcuts to execute different actions based on specific conditions or variables.

- o **Parameter Inputs**: Customize shortcut behaviours by prompting for user input or extracting data from previous actions.

- **Examples**:

  - o **Dynamic Content**: Create shortcuts that adapt based on current data, such as fetching the latest weather information or updating shopping lists.

  - o **Interactive Shortcuts**: Use interactive components to confirm actions, choose options, or provide additional information during execution.

6. Sharing and Discovering Shortcuts

- **Sharing Shortcuts**:

  - o **Public Links**: Share your created shortcuts with others via links or AirDrop for collaborative productivity.

  - o **Gallery and Discover**:

    - ▪ **Explore**: Discover new shortcuts through the Shortcuts Gallery, featuring curated collections and user-submitted shortcuts.

    - ▪ **Community Contribution**: Contribute to the community by sharing your own shortcuts and exploring what others have created.

7. Privacy and Security

- **Data Handling**:

  - o **On-Device Processing**: Shortcuts execute most tasks locally on your device to prioritize user privacy and minimize reliance on external servers.

  - o **Encryption and Permissions**: Ensure sensitive information remains secure through encrypted communications and user-permissioned data access.

8. Integration with HomeKit and Third-Party Apps

- **Smart Home Automation**:

    o **HomeKit Support**: Control smart home devices and create automation routines using Siri Shortcuts.

    o **App Integrations**: Extend shortcut capabilities by integrating with third-party apps, enhancing device control and task automation.

9. Continued Learning and Updates

- **AI Advancements**:

    o **Machine Learning**: Siri Shortcuts evolve with user interactions and feedback, improving performance and expanding functionality over time.

Regular Updates: Receive updates from Apple to introduce new actions, optimize performance, and add support for additional apps and services.

Core Apps and Features

Messages and FaceTime

New Features in Messages for iOS 18

Messages offers more capabilities for

iPhone shows a message being composed with the word "bouncing" selected and the text effect Jitter selected.1. Enhanced Group Chats

- **Threaded Conversations**:
  - ○ **Organized Threads**: Messages now organize group conversations into threaded threads, making it easier to follow multiple discussions within the same chat.
  - ○ **Reply Threads**: Respond directly to specific messages within a thread to keep conversations clear and focused.
- **Mentions**:

- o **Tagging Individuals**: Mention specific group members using @mentions to draw their attention to relevant messages or topics.

- o **Notifications**: Users receive notifications when mentioned, ensuring important messages are seen promptly.

2. Live Stickers and Effects

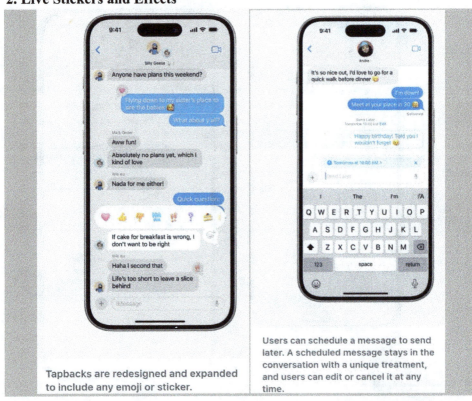

Tapbacks are redesigned and expanded to include any emoji or sticker.

Users can schedule a message to send later. A scheduled message stays in the conversation with a unique treatment, and users can edit or cancel it at any time.

Shows an iMessage selected with Tapback options, including a heart, thumbs-up, thumbs-down, haha, exclamation point, question mark, and cake emoji.

- o **Live Stickers**: Send and receive animated stickers that react to user interactions, adding fun and expression to conversations.

- o **Effects**: Apply visual effects to messages, such as balloons, confetti, or fireworks, to celebrate special occasions or emphasize messages.

3. Message Effects

- **Dynamic Backgrounds**: Choose from a variety of dynamic backgrounds for your messages, including live backgrounds that react to touch and movement.

- **Customization**: Personalize messages with animated effects and themes to match your mood or the occasion.

4. Advanced Privacy Features

- **End-to-end Encryption**: Messages continue to prioritize user privacy with end-to-end encryption, ensuring that only intended recipients can access message content.

- **Private Replies**: Send replies privately in group chats without disrupting the main conversation thread, maintaining confidentiality.

5. Message Effects

- **Bubble Effects**: Use bubble effects like slam, loud, gentle, and invisible ink to add emphasis or surprise to your messages.

- **Screen Effects**: Celebrate special moments with screen effects such as balloons, confetti, fireworks, and more, which animate across the recipient's screen.

6. Message Reactions

- **Tapbacks**: React quickly to messages using Tapbacks, which include emojis like thumbs up, thumbs down, hearts, and more.

- **Personalization**: Customize Tapbacks to convey your sentiment with a single tap, enhancing communication efficiency.

7. Integration with Other Apple Services

- **SharePlay Integration**: Seamlessly share media and collaborate on apps during FaceTime calls directly from Messages.

- **Apple Pay**: Send and receive money securely through Messages using Apple Pay, integrating financial transactions into your messaging experience.

Users get new ways to pay with Apple Pay, including the ability to redeem rewards and access installments from their eligible credit or debit cards.

- *With Tap to Cash, users can send and receive Apple Cash by holding two iPhone devices together.*

8. Smart Delivery and Read Receipts

o **Delivery Notifications**: See when your message has been delivered to the recipient's device.

o **Read Receipts**: View when messages are read by the recipient, providing clarity on message status and interaction.

9. Personalization and Customization

o **Theme Packs**: Access a variety of theme packs to customize message backgrounds, fonts, and colours.

- o **Animated Emojis**: Send animated emojis and Memojis that react to your facial expressions and gestures, enhancing personalization.

Enhancements in FaceTime for iOS 18

iOS 18 brings a variety of enhancements to FaceTime, Apple's popular video and audio calling app, enhancing communication and collaboration with new features designed to make conversations more immersive, engaging, and secure. Here's an overview of the key enhancements in FaceTime:

1. Spatial Audio

- o **Spatial Sound**: Spatial audio simulates a surround sound experience, making voices and sounds feel as if they're coming from different directions.

- o **Dynamic Panning**: Audio dynamically adjusts as participants speak or move, enhancing realism and clarity during calls.

2. SharePlay Enhancements

- o **Media Sharing**: Share movies, TV shows, music, and other media in real-time during FaceTime calls.

- o **App Sharing**: Collaborate on apps together, such as browsing through photos, planning trips, or working on documents simultaneously.

3. Grid View and Focus Modes

o **Grid View**: See all participants in a call at once with the grid view layout, making it easier to follow conversations with multiple people.

o **Focus Modes**: Highlight the active speaker or content being shared to keep attention on the most relevant participant or information.

4. Portrait Mode

o **Blur Backgrounds**: Portrait mode blurs the background during FaceTime calls, focusing attention on the caller and reducing distractions.

o **Enhanced Video Quality**: Improve video clarity and aesthetics with a professional-looking depth-of-field effect.

5. Improved Call Management

o **Mic Modes**: Choose between voice isolation or wide spectrum modes to optimize audio quality based on your environment.

o **Camera Controls**: Easily switch between front and back cameras, mute audio, or disable video during calls for privacy and convenience.

6. Integration with Messages and Notifications

o **Message Integration**: Continue conversations from Messages directly into FaceTime calls, ensuring smooth transitions between text and video interactions.

o **Notification Controls**: Manage FaceTime call notifications, including scheduling and reminders, to stay informed about upcoming calls.

7. Live Photos and Memories

o **Live Photos**: Capture spontaneous moments during FaceTime calls with Live Photos, saving them directly to your Photos library for sharing and memories.

o **Shared Albums**: Automatically curate and share photos and videos from FaceTime calls in personalized albums, preserving memories and experiences.

8. Enhanced Privacy and Security

o **End-to-end Encryption**: FaceTime calls remain private and secure with end-to-end encryption, ensuring that only participants can access conversation content.

o **Granular Controls**: Manage privacy settings, including who can join calls and how notifications are handled, to maintain control over your communications.

9. Accessibility Features

o **VoiceOver Compatibility**: Ensure FaceTime is accessible to users with visual impairments through VoiceOver, providing audio descriptions and controls.

o **Closed Captions**: Enable closed captions during calls to improve communication for users with hearing impairments.

Use SharePlay and Other Collaboration Tools

iOS 18 introduces SharePlay and a suite of collaboration tools that enhance how users interact and share experiences in real-time during FaceTime calls and other supported apps. These features facilitate seamless collaboration, entertainment, and productivity, making it easier to connect and engage with others remotely:

1. SharePlay

o **Media Sharing**: Share movies, TV shows, music, and more with participants during FaceTime calls.

o **App Sharing**: Collaborate on apps together, such as browsing through photos, planning trips, or working on documents simultaneously.

• **How to Use SharePlay**:

o **Initiating SharePlay**: Start a FaceTime call and select the media or app you want to share. Tap the SharePlay button to invite participants to join and synchronize the experience.

o **Media Playback**: Enjoy synchronized playback of shared media, with playback controls accessible to all participants.

o **App Interaction**: Interact with shared apps in real-time, allowing everyone to view and contribute to activities like editing documents or browsing content.

2. Collaboration Tools

o **Supported Apps**: Utilize collaboration features in supported third-party apps, enhancing productivity and creativity during shared sessions.

o **API Integration**: Developers can integrate SharePlay into their apps, expanding functionality and use cases across various categories.

3. Integration with Messages

o **Message Integration**: Easily transition from text conversations in Messages to FaceTime calls with SharePlay, ensuring continuity and efficiency in communication.

o **Notification Controls**: Manage notifications and reminders for scheduled SharePlay sessions, ensuring participants are informed and ready to join.

4. Privacy and Security

o **End-to-end Encryption**: SharePlay sessions are protected with end-to-end encryption, safeguarding shared media and app interactions from unauthorized access.

o **Participant Control**: Manage participants and session controls, including who can join, share content, and interact during SharePlay sessions.

5. Accessibility Features

o **Accessibility Support**: Ensure SharePlay is accessible to users with disabilities through features like VoiceOver compatibility and closed captions.

o **Customization Options**: Tailor SharePlay settings to accommodate diverse needs and preferences, promoting inclusivity in collaborative experiences.

6. Enhanced User Experience

- o **Visual Feedback**: View participant reactions and interactions in real-time, enhancing engagement and communication during shared activities.

- o **Enhanced Connectivity**: Enjoy seamless connectivity and synchronization across devices, ensuring a smooth and uninterrupted collaborative experience.

7. Future Developments and Updates

- o **Feature Expansion**: Expect future updates to introduce new SharePlay capabilities, integration with additional apps, and enhanced collaboration tools based on user feedback and technological advancements.

- o **Developer Opportunities**: Explore opportunities for developers to innovate and integrate SharePlay into their apps, expanding functionality and use cases for users worldwide.

1. Mail, Calendar, and Contacts

- o Organizing and managing email
- o Calendar improvements and tips
- o Integrating and managing contacts

2. Safari and Browsing

- o New features in Safari

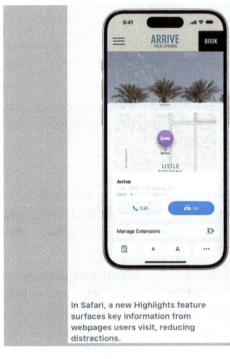

In Safari, a new Highlights feature surfaces key information from webpages users visit, reducing distractions.

Reader in Safari has been redesigned to help users enjoy articles by including a summary and a table of contents.

..displays an article titled "Can Meditation Change Your Mind" with a summary and table of contents shown.

- ○ Managing tabs and bookmarks
- ○ Privacy and security settings

3. **Photos and Camera**

   - ○ Using the Camera app and new photography features

   - ○ Organizing and editing photos
   - ○ Sharing and syncing across devices

Settings and Customization

General Settings

Overview of the Settings App

The Settings app in iOS 18 serves as the control centre for customizing and managing various aspects of your iPhone's functionality, preferences, and security. It provides users with access to a wide range of options to personalize their devices, adjust system settings, manage accounts, and ensure privacy:

1. General Settings

- Access details about your iPhone, including model, capacity, software version, and carrier information.

- **Legal & Regulatory**: View regulatory information, legal notices, and certifications related to your device.

- **Software Update**:

  - **Automatic Updates**: Enable or disable automatic updates for iOS and installed apps to ensure your device is up to date with the latest features and security patches.

- **Accessibility**:

  - **Accessibility Features**: Customize settings for vision, hearing, mobility, and cognitive accessibility needs, ensuring the device is accessible to all users.

2. Wireless & Networks

- **Network Selection**: Connect to available Wi-Fi networks, manage saved networks, and configure network settings for seamless internet connectivity.

- **Bluetooth**:

  - **Device Pairing**: Pair and manage Bluetooth-enabled devices such as headphones, speakers, keyboards, and smart home accessories for wireless connectivity.

- **Cellular**:

- o **Data Usage**: Monitor cellular data usage, manage cellular plans, and configure data roaming settings to optimize usage and control costs.

3. Personalization and Customization

- **Wallpaper**:

  - o **Home Screen and Lock Screen**: Change wallpaper images for the Home Screen and Lock Screen, including dynamic and static options.

- **Sounds & Haptics**:

  - o **Ringtone and Alerts**: Customize ringtone, alert tones, and vibration patterns for calls, messages, and notifications based on personal preferences.

- **Display & Brightness**:

  - o **Brightness Adjustment**: Adjust screen brightness, enable Night Shift for reduced blue light emission at night, and configure auto-lock settings to conserve battery.

4. Privacy and Security

- **Privacy**:

  - o **App Permissions**: Manage permissions for apps to access sensitive data such as location, contacts, photos, and microphone, ensuring user privacy and data security.

- **Security**:

  - o **Passcode and Face/Touch ID**: Set up and manage device security with passcode settings, Face ID, or Touch ID for secure authentication and access control.

5. Applications and Notifications

- **Notifications**:

  - o **Notification Center**: Customize notification settings for each app, including alerts, banners, sounds, and grouping preferences to manage incoming notifications efficiently.

- **App Store**:

- o **Automatic Downloads**: Configure settings for automatic downloads of app updates, purchases, and subscriptions across all devices linked to your Apple ID.

6. Account Settings

- **Apple ID**:

  - o **Account Information**: Manage your Apple ID profile, payment methods, subscriptions, and family-sharing settings for seamless integration across Apple services.

- **iCloud**:

  - o **Storage and Backup**: Manage iCloud storage, and backup settings, and synchronize data such as photos, contacts, calendars, and documents across devices.

7. Device and Battery Management

- **Battery**:

  - o **Battery Health**: Monitor battery usage, view battery health information, and optimize battery settings to extend device battery life and performance.

- **Storage**:

  - o **Manage Storage**: View detailed storage usage, manage storage settings, and optimize device storage by deleting unused apps, files, and data.

8. Advanced Settings

- **VPN and Network Settings**:

  - o **VPN Configuration**: Configure virtual private networks (VPNs) for secure internet browsing and network access, ensuring data privacy and protection.

- **Developer Options**:

  - o **Developer Settings**: Access advanced options for developers, including debugging tools, USB connectivity settings, and app performance monitoring.

9. System and Maintenance

- o **Reset Options**: Reset device settings, and network settings, or erase all content and settings for troubleshooting or preparing the device for resale.

- o **Software Update**: Configure software update preferences, download updates, and manage installation schedules to keep the device up to date with the latest iOS version.

10. Legal Notices: View legal disclaimers, terms of use, and regulatory information related to iOS and Apple services for compliance and reference purposes.

Device Management and Information

In iOS 18, managing your device and accessing essential information is facilitated through the Settings app, offering users a centralized hub to customize settings, monitor performance, and ensure security:

1. General Device Information

- **About**

  - o **Device Model and Name**: View detailed information about your iPhone, including the model, capacity, serial number, and IMEI/MEID.

  - o **Software Version**: Check the current iOS version installed and verify if updates are available for installation.

  - o **Carrier Details**: Access information regarding your cellular carrier, network status, and other relevant details.

2. Software Updates

- **Software Update**

  - o **Automatic Updates**: Enable or disable automatic updates to ensure your device remains up to date with the latest iOS features, security patches, and bug fixes.

  - o **Update History**: Review past updates and changes introduced in each iOS version, including improvements and new functionalities.

3. Battery and Performance

- **Battery**

  - **Battery Health**: Monitor the health of your iPhone's battery, checking its maximum capacity and peak performance capability over time.

  - **Usage Statistics**: View detailed usage statistics to understand how apps and activities impact battery life, and optimize settings to conserve power.

4. Storage Management

- **iPhone Storage**

  - **Storage Overview**: See a breakdown of used and available storage space on your device, including recommendations for optimizing storage by deleting unused apps, photos, and files.

  - **App Management**: Manage app storage individually, including offloading apps to reclaim storage space while retaining app data.

5. Privacy and Security Settings

- **Privacy**

  - **App Permissions**: Review and manage permissions granted to apps for accessing sensitive data such as location, contacts, photos, microphone, and camera.

  - **Tracking Controls**: Configure settings related to app tracking transparency, allowing users to control which apps can track their activity across other apps and websites.

6. Network and Connectivity

- **Wi-Fi and Bluetooth**

  - **Network Settings**: Manage Wi-Fi networks and Bluetooth devices, including connecting to new networks, forgetting saved networks, and pairing new Bluetooth devices.

  - **Personal Hotspot**: Enable or disable the personal hotspot feature to share your iPhone's internet connection with other devices via Wi-Fi, Bluetooth, or USB.

7. Accessibility Features

- **Accessibility**

  - **Accessibility Settings**: Customize accessibility features tailored to your specific needs, including vision, hearing, mobility, and cognitive accessibility options.

  - **AssistiveTouch**: Activate AssistiveTouch for alternative touch controls, gestures, and shortcuts to enhance device usability.

8. Security and Privacy

- **Face ID/Touch ID and Passcode**

  - **Biometric Authentication**: Manage settings for Face ID or Touch ID for secure device unlocking and authentication of purchases, passwords, and sensitive data.

  - **Passcode Settings**: Configure passcode settings, including passcode length, complexity requirements, and automatic lock intervals to protect device access.

9. Advanced Settings and System

- **Reset**

  - **Reset Options**: Perform device resets, including resetting all settings, and network settings, or erasing all content and settings to troubleshoot issues or prepare the device for resale.

  - **Emergency SOS**: Set up and configure emergency SOS settings for quick access to emergency services and contacts in critical situations.

10. Support and Legal Information

- **Support**

  - **Contact Support**: Access Apple Support options for troubleshooting, repairs, and technical assistance related to your iPhone and Apple services.

  - **Legal & Regulatory**: Review legal notices, terms of use, and regulatory information regarding iOS, Apple services, and consumer rights.

Accessibility Features

iOS 18 continues to prioritize accessibility with a comprehensive range of features designed to make iPhone usage more inclusive and accessible to users with diverse needs. These features empower individuals with disabilities to navigate, interact, and utilize their devices effectively:

1. Vision Accessibility

- **VoiceOver**

  - **Screen Reader**: Provides audible descriptions of what's on the screen, enabling users with visual impairments to navigate apps, read text, and interact with content.

  - **Braille Display Support**: Connects to compatible Braille displays for tactile feedback and enhanced accessibility in reading and interacting with device content.

- **Magnifier**

  - **Digital Magnification**: Use the iPhone camera to magnify text, objects, and images in real time, with options for enhanced contrast and brightness adjustments.

- **Display Accommodations**

  - **Colour Filters**: Customize display colours to improve visibility for users with colour blindness or sensitivity to certain colours.

  - **Invert Colors and Grayscale**: Invert colours or enable grayscale mode for reduced visual stimulation and improved readability.

2. Hearing Accessibility

- **Live Listen**

  - **Audio Support**: Amplifies sound captured by the iPhone's microphone, transmitting it directly to compatible hearing aids or AirPods for enhanced listening experiences in noisy environments.

- **Sound Recognition**

- o **Alerts for Recognized Sounds**: Notifies users of important sounds such as doorbells, sirens, or alarms, enhancing situational awareness for individuals with hearing impairments.

3. Physical and Motor Skills Accessibility

- **AssistiveTouch**

  - o **Alternative Controls**: Enables customizable gestures, virtual buttons, and shortcuts to assist users with physical disabilities in navigating and interacting with their devices.

- **Switch Control**

  - o **Scanning Options**: Allows control of the iPhone using adaptive switches or Bluetooth-enabled devices, providing users with limited mobility and more flexibility in device interaction.

4. Communication Accessibility

- **Speech**

  - o **Text-to-Speech (Speak Screen)**: Converts on-screen text into spoken words, facilitating reading and accessibility for users with dyslexia or other reading challenges.

- **Voice Control**

  - o **Voice Commands**: Navigate and control the iPhone entirely by voice, including launching apps, dictating messages, and performing actions, supporting hands-free interaction.

5. Interaction and Navigation

- **Siri**

  - o **Voice Assistant**: Use voice commands to perform tasks, retrieve information, and control device functions, offering a hands-free alternative for accessing device features.

- **Guided Access**

  - o **App Limitations**: Restrict the iPhone to a single app, control touch interactions, and limit access to certain features, ideal for users needing focused attention or educational settings.

6. Inclusive Design and Customization

- **Accessibility Shortcuts**

    - **Quick Access**: Set up shortcuts to activate frequently used accessibility features with ease, such as enabling VoiceOver or Magnifier with a triple-click of the side button.

- **Text Size and Font Adjustment**

    - **Text Customization**: Adjust text size, font style, and boldness to improve readability and accommodate visual preferences.

Privacy and Security

Enhanced Privacy Settings in iOS 18

Privacy remains a top priority in iOS 18, offering users robust tools and settings to safeguard personal information, control app permissions, and manage data transparency. These enhanced privacy features empower users to protect their digital footprint and maintain confidentiality while using their iPhones:

For times when a user shares their device with someone and wants peace of mind that private information remains unseen, apps can be locked with Face ID, Touch ID, or the device passcode, and information from these

Locked apps can be hidden in a dedicated folder in the App Library so they don't appear on the Home Screen.

iPhone shows a screen with a prompt asking if the user would like to require Face ID for the Photos app; another reveals a screen with a prompt asking if the user would like to hide an app called Treble Threat.

1. App Privacy Reports

- **Comprehensive Insights**:
    - **Detailed Reports**: Provides users with detailed insights into how apps use their data, including which apps have accessed sensitive information such as location, camera, microphone, contacts, and more.
    - **Weekly Summary**: Receive a weekly summary of app activity and data usage to stay informed about potential privacy concerns.

2. Tracking Transparency

- **App Tracking Transparency**:
    - **User Consent**: Requires apps to request user permission before tracking their activity across other apps and websites for targeted advertising purposes.
    - **App Privacy Details**: View detailed information on how apps use tracking data and manage permissions in Settings to control app tracking preferences.

3. Location Services

- **Precise Control**:
    - **App Permissions**: Manage location permissions for each app individually, allowing users to grant access to precise location data, approximate location, or disable location services entirely.
    - **Background Location Notifications**: Receive notifications when apps access location data in the background, ensuring transparency and control over location tracking.

4. Photos and Camera

- **Privacy Controls**:
    - **Access Permissions**: Manage app permissions for accessing photos and camera, granting selective access to media files only when necessary for app functionality.

- o **On-device Processing**: Emphasizes on-device processing for camera and photo editing apps to enhance privacy by minimizing data exposure to third-party servers.

5. Microphone and Audio

- **Microphone Access**:

  - o **Indicator and Permissions**: Display an indicator whenever an app accesses the microphone, providing users with awareness and control over audio recording permissions.

  - o **Control Permissions**: Manage app permissions to grant or revoke access to the microphone, ensuring apps only capture audio when authorized.

6. Safari and Browser Privacy

- **Enhanced Tracking Prevention**:

  - o **Intelligent Tracking Prevention**: Mitigates cross-site tracking by limiting advertisers' ability to track user activity across websites, enhancing privacy while browsing with Safari.

  - o **Privacy Report**: View a summary of blocked trackers and monitor website privacy practices to understand how Safari protects user data.

7. Secure Sign-in and Authentication

- **Sign in with Apple**:

  - o **Anonymous Email Forwarding**: Provides users with the option to use an anonymized email address when signing in to apps and websites, protecting personal email addresses from exposure.

  - o **Two-Factor Authentication**: Secure accounts with an additional layer of protection through two-factor authentication (2FA) to prevent unauthorized access.

8. Data Access and Control

- **Data Transparency**:

  - o **Manage App Permissions**: Access settings to review and manage permissions granted to apps for accessing sensitive data, ensuring users maintain control over their personal information.

- o **Data Minimization**: Promotes data minimization practices, encouraging developers to collect and process only essential user data necessary for app functionality.

9. Privacy Settings and Transparency

- **Transparency and Control**:
  - o **Clear Privacy Labels**: Display clear, standardized privacy labels on the App Store to inform users about app privacy practices before downloading or purchasing apps.

  - o **Educational Resources**: Provide educational resources and guidelines for developers to prioritize user privacy and comply with Apple's App Store policies.

Advanced Features

Cloud and Storage Management

In iOS 18, iCloud and storage management tools provide users with efficient ways to store, access, and manage their data across Apple devices.

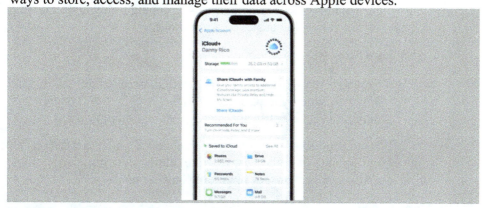

From iCloud storage optimization to file management, these features ensure seamless integration and secure data handling:

1. iCloud Overview

- o **Automatic Backup**: Automatically backs up photos, videos, app data, device settings, and more to iCloud, ensuring data preservation and easy restoration.

- o **Sync Across Devices**: Synchronize data, including contacts, calendars, reminders, and documents, across all Apple devices linked to the same iCloud account for seamless access.

2. iCloud Storage Management

- o **Storage Plans**: Choose from various iCloud storage plans (5 GB free, with options for additional storage up to 2 TB) to accommodate different storage needs and preferences.

- o **Upgrade and Downgrade**: Easily upgrade or downgrade iCloud storage plans as needed, with prorated billing adjustments based on usage and plan changes.

3. Optimize Storage

- o **Offload Unused Apps**: Automatically removes rarely used apps while preserving app data, reclaiming storage space on the device without losing essential data.

- o **Photos and Videos**: Optimize storage by storing full-resolution photos and videos in iCloud while keeping lightweight versions on the device to conserve local storage.

4. Manage iCloud Storage

- o **Storage Breakdown**: View detailed breakdowns of iCloud storage usage by app, photos, videos, backups, and documents, helping users identify and manage storage-hungry items.

- o **Recommendations**: Receive personalized recommendations for optimizing storage usage, including deleting large files, managing backups, or upgrading storage plans.

5. File Management

- o **Unified Access**: Access and manage files stored in iCloud Drive and other cloud storage services directly from the Files app, supporting file organization and sharing.

- o **Tagging and Searching**: Organize files with tags, perform advanced searches, and access recent files across devices for streamlined file management.

6. Collaboration and Sharing

- o **Collaborative Spaces**: Create shared albums and folders in iCloud Photos and iCloud Drive, allowing multiple users to collaborate, share, and edit documents in real time.

- o **File Sharing Controls**: Manage permissions and control access to shared files and folders, ensuring secure collaboration while protecting data privacy.

7. Backup and Restore

- o **Automatic Backups**: Ensure continuous data protection with automatic iCloud backups, enabling seamless restoration of data in case of device loss, damage, or upgrade.

- o **Restore Options**: Restore device settings, apps, and data from iCloud backups during device setup or after resetting the device to factory settings.

8. Privacy and Security

- o **Data Protection**: Secure data stored in iCloud with end-to-end encryption, ensuring that only authorized devices and users can access and decrypt stored information.

- o **Two-Factor Authentication**: Enhance account security with two-factor authentication (2FA), adding an extra layer of protection for iCloud and Apple ID access.

App Store and App Management

The App Store in iOS 18 serves as a gateway to a vast ecosystem of apps, offering users access to a wide range of applications for productivity, entertainment, utilities, and more. iOS 18 enhances the App Store experience with improved app discovery, security, and management features:

1. App Discovery and Updates

- o **Featured and Explore Tabs**: Discover new apps, games, and collections curated by Apple editors, highlighting top picks and trending content.

- o **Search and Suggestions**: Easily find apps using intuitive search functionality with autocomplete suggestions and filters by category, ratings, and relevance.

- o **Updates**: Enable automatic updates for apps to ensure they are always up to date with the latest features, bug fixes, and security patches.

- o **Update History**: View a history of app updates, including release notes and changes introduced in each update.

2. App Installation and Management

- o **Install and Uninstall**: Download and install apps directly from the App Store, with options to uninstall apps to free up storage space when necessary.

- o **App Store Purchases**: Access a history of purchased apps and download them again at no additional cost on new or restored devices linked to the same Apple ID.

- o **App Privacy Details**: View privacy labels on each app listing to understand how apps collect and use data before downloading.

- o **App Permissions**: Manage app permissions for location, camera, microphone, contacts, and more directly from the app settings in iOS 18.

3. App Store Settings

- o **App Updates and Purchases**: Customize settings for automatic downloads of app updates, purchases, and subscriptions across all devices linked to your Apple ID.

- o Manage payment methods, add or remove credit cards, and update billing information for App Store purchases and subscriptions.

- o **Family Sharing**: Share purchased apps, subscriptions, and iCloud storage with family members using Family Sharing, ensuring shared access and control over family purchases.

4. App Ratings and Reviews

- o **Ratings and Reviews**: Read and contribute ratings and reviews for apps to help other users make informed decisions before downloading.

- o **Developer Responses**: View developer responses to user reviews, providing additional context and support for app feedback and concerns.

5. App Store Guidelines and Policies

- o **App Store Review Guidelines**: Access guidelines and policies for developers to ensure app compliance with Apple's quality standards, security protocols, and content guidelines.

- o **App Store Submissions**: Submit apps for review and approval by Apple to ensure they meet App Store requirements before being made available to users.

6. In-app purchases and Subscriptions

- o **Manage Subscriptions**: View and manage active app subscriptions, including renewal options, upgrade/downgrade plans, and cancellations directly from the App Store settings.

7. App Store Security

- o **App Authenticity**: Ensure app authenticity and security with secure downloads from the App Store, protecting against unauthorized or malicious software installations.

8. Educational Resources and Support

- o **Developer Insights**: Access educational resources, developer forums, and technical support to assist in app development, optimization, and compliance with App Store guidelines.

Health and Fitness

iOS 18 introduces a variety of innovative features designed to enhance health and fitness tracking, providing users with tools to monitor and improve their overall well-being:

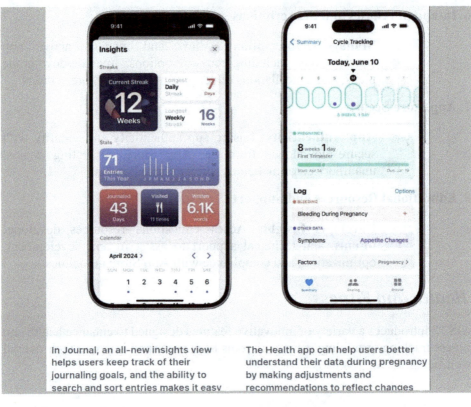

In Journal, an all-new insights view helps users keep track of their journaling goals, and the ability to search and sort entries makes it easy

The Health app can help users better understand their data during pregnancy by making adjustments and recommendations to reflect changes

1. Activity Tracking

- o Track daily steps, distance travelled, and active minutes using the iPhone's built-in sensors.
- o Monitor progress towards daily activity goals and receive notifications to stay motivated.

- **Workout Tracking**:

  - o Choose from a variety of workout types, including running, cycling, yoga, and more.
  - o Access real-time metrics such as heart rate, pace, and calories burned during workouts.

2. Health Dashboard

- o View a consolidated dashboard displaying health metrics such as steps, exercise minutes, heart rate trends, and sleep patterns.

- o Receive personalized recommendations based on health data to achieve fitness goals.

3. Sleep Tracking

- o Monitor sleep duration and quality using data collected from the iPhone's accelerometer and gyroscope.
- o Receive insights into sleep patterns and suggestions for improving sleep hygiene.

4. Mindfulness and Stress Management

- o Access guided breathing exercises and meditation sessions to reduce stress and improve mental well-being.
- o Track mindfulness minutes and monitor trends in relaxation and stress reduction.

5. Nutrition Tracking

- o meals and track nutritional intake, including calories, macronutrients (carbohydrates, proteins, fats), and micronutrients.
- o Use barcode scanning and database search to easily add foods and beverages to the log.

6. Heart Rate Monitoring

- o Monitor resting and active heart rate throughout the day to assess cardiovascular health.
- o Receive alerts for abnormal heart rates and trends that may indicate potential health concerns.

7. Medical ID and Emergency Features

- o Store critical health information such as allergies, medical conditions, medications, and emergency contacts.
- o Access Medical ID from the lock screen for quick reference during emergencies.

8. Health Records Integration

- o Integrate health records from healthcare providers to view lab results, immunizations, medications, and other medical information securely.

- o Receive notifications for new health record updates and share records with healthcare professionals as needed.

9. Data Privacy and Security

- o Ensure all health and fitness data is encrypted and stored securely on the device and in iCloud.

- o Manage data-sharing permissions with third-party apps and healthcare providers to maintain privacy.

10. Health Research Participation

- o Participate in health research studies and contribute anonymized data to advance medical research and public health initiatives.

- o Access insights from aggregated health data to gain a deeper understanding of personal health trends and contribute to global health research.

Connectivity and Integration

Connect with Other Devices

In iOS 18, Apple continues to enhance connectivity features, allowing users to seamlessly connect and interact with various devices, including other Apple devices, smart accessories, and third-party gadgets:

1. Apple Ecosystem Integration

- **Continuity and Handoff**:
    - Seamlessly transition tasks between iPhone, iPad, Mac, and Apple Watch with Handoff.
    - Pick up where you left off in apps, emails, messages, Safari browsing sessions, and more across devices.

- **Universal Clipboard**:
    - Copy text, images, and files on one Apple device and paste them on another using Universal Clipboard.
    - Ensure smooth workflow integration between iPhone, iPad, and Mac devices.

2. AirDrop

- **File Sharing**:
    - Share photos, videos, documents, and other files wirelessly with nearby Apple devices using AirDrop.
    - Securely transfer files between iPhone, iPad, and Mac without requiring internet connectivity.

3. Apple Watch Connectivity

- **Health and Fitness Integration**:
    - Sync health and fitness data between iPhone and Apple Watch for comprehensive activity tracking and analysis.
    - Receive notifications, alerts, and health insights on the wrist through seamless device synchronization.

4. HomeKit and Smart Home Integration

- **Control Smart Devices**:
    - Manage and control smart home devices compatible with HomeKit directly from the iPhone.
    - Set up automation routines, adjust settings, and monitor device status remotely using the Home app.

5. CarPlay

- **In-Vehicle Integration**:
    - Connect iPhone to CarPlay-enabled vehicles for enhanced in-car entertainment, navigation, communication, and Siri voice control.
    - Access apps, music, messages, and maps with a simplified interface optimized for driving.

6. Bluetooth and Wi-Fi Connectivity

- **Peripheral Device Pairing**:
    - Pair the iPhone with Bluetooth-enabled devices such as headphones, speakers, keyboards, and game controllers for wireless audio and data transfer.
    - Connect to Wi-Fi networks seamlessly for internet access and data sharing.

7. Third-Party Accessories

- **Compatibility**:
    - Connect and interact with a wide range of third-party accessories and peripherals through Bluetooth, Wi-Fi, and proprietary connectors.
    - Enjoy expanded functionality and features provided by accessories designed for iOS compatibility.

8. Integration with External Displays

- **Screen Mirroring**:

- o Mirror iPhone screen to compatible external displays, TVs, and projectors using AirPlay or HDMI adapters for presentations, gaming, and media playback.

- o Extend or duplicate the iPhone screen for enhanced productivity and entertainment purposes.

Home and Smart Devices

iOS 18 continues to enhance the integration and management of smart home devices, providing users with a centralized platform to control and automate their home environment efficiently:

1. Home App Overview

- **Centralized Control**:
  - o Use the Home app as a central hub to manage and control all HomeKit-compatible smart home devices. Access devices such as lights, thermostats, cameras, door locks, and more from a single interface.

- **Room Organization**:
  - o Organize devices by rooms and zones within the Home app for intuitive navigation and control. Create custom scenes to automate multiple devices with a single command or schedule.

2. Smart Home Automation

- **Automated Scenes and Routines**:
  - o Create personalized scenes and automation routines based on time of day, location triggers, or device interactions. Automate actions like adjusting lighting, temperature, and security settings to suit daily routines.

3. Voice Control with Siri

- **Voice-Activated Commands**:
  - o Control HomeKit devices using voice commands with Siri integration. Use natural language to adjust settings, activate scenes, and query device status hands-free.

4. Security and Notifications

- **Real-time Alerts**:
  - Receive notifications and alerts from connected smart devices, such as motion detection, doorbell rings, or smoke alarms. Monitor home security cameras and doorbell cameras directly from the Home app.

5. Remote Access

- **Access Anywhere**:
  - Control and monitor home devices remotely over Wi-Fi or cellular data. Ensure peace of mind with remote access to security cameras, door locks, and sensors while away from home.

6. Apple TV and HomePod Integration

- **Hub Functionality**:
  - Use Apple TV or HomePod as a home hub to enable remote access and automation for HomeKit devices. Ensure devices remain connected and responsive even when away from home.

7. Energy Efficiency

- **Energy Monitoring**:
  - Monitor and track the energy consumption of smart home devices to optimize usage and reduce energy costs. Receive insights into energy usage patterns and recommendations for efficiency improvements.

8. Compatibility with Third-Party Devices

- **Expanded Device Support**:
  - Integrate and control a wide range of third-party smart home devices and accessories compatible with HomeKit. Enjoy seamless interoperability and enhanced functionality through iOS 18's ecosystem.

CarPlay and External Displays

The CarPlay experience and support for external displays, provides users with seamless integration, and improved navigation, communication, and entertainment options while on the move:

1. CarPlay Overview

- **In-Vehicle Integration**:
  - Connect the iPhone to a CarPlay-compatible vehicle to access a simplified interface on the vehicle's display. Control essential iPhone functions via the car's touchscreen, knobs, or voice commands for safer and more convenient driving.

2. Features of CarPlay

- **Navigation and Maps**:Apple Intelligence Transforms the iPhone Experience

Apple Intelligence unlocks new ways for users to enhance their writing and communicate more effectively.

In Apple Maps, users can browse thousands of hikes across national parks in the United States and easily create their own custom walking routes, which they can still access offline.

iPhone displays a message being composed with Writing Tools below it, including proofreading and rewrite options.

- o Use Apple Maps or supported third-party navigation apps for turn-by-turn directions, real-time traffic updates, and predictive routing. Access navigation prompts directly on the car's display with voice-guided directions.

- **Communication**:
  - o Make and receive calls hands-free using Siri voice commands or the car's controls. Send and listen to messages, dictating replies without taking your hands off the wheel.

- **Music and Entertainment**:
  - o Access your favourite music, podcasts, audiobooks, and streaming apps directly through CarPlay. Enjoy personalized playlists, recommendations, and controls for playback and volume adjustments.

3. Siri Integration

- **Voice Commands**:
  - o Use Siri voice commands to control CarPlay functions, including navigation, communication, and entertainment. Stay focused on the road while accessing information and performing tasks using natural language.

4. Third-Party App Support

- **App Integration**:
  - o Access supported third-party apps via CarPlay for additional functionality and personalized content. Enjoy enhanced app experiences tailored for driving, such as news updates, weather forecasts, and smart home controls.

5. CarPlay Dashboard

- **Customizable Interface**:
  - o Customize the CarPlay dashboard to display preferred apps, widgets, and shortcuts for quick access while driving. Manage navigation, music, messages, and other apps from a single screen optimized for minimal distraction.

6. External Display Support

- **Screen Mirroring**:
    - Mirror iPhone screen to compatible external displays, TVs, or projectors using AirPlay or HDMI adapters.
    - Extend iPhone display for presentations, gaming, multimedia playback, and productivity tasks on larger screens.

7. Compatibility and Performance

- **Device Compatibility**:
    - Ensure seamless compatibility with CarPlay-enabled vehicles and external displays supporting AirPlay or HDMI connectivity.
    - Experience optimized performance for smooth navigation, multimedia playback, and app interaction across supported devices.

Troubleshooting and Maintenance

Common Issues and Solutions

iOS 18 aims to provide a seamless user experience, but occasionally users may encounter issues. Here's an outline of common issues and their solutions:

1. Battery Drain

- **Issue**: Rapid battery drain or shortened battery life after updating to iOS 18.

- **Solution**:

  o **Check Battery Usage**: Go to Settings > Battery to identify apps consuming excessive power. Consider closing background apps or adjusting settings to optimize battery usage.

  o **Update Apps**: Ensure all apps are updated to their latest versions, as older versions may not be optimized for iOS 18.

  o **Restart or Reset**: Restart your device or perform a soft reset by holding down the Power button and Home button (for older models) or Power button and Volume Down button (for newer models) until the Apple logo appears.

2. Wi-Fi and Connectivity Issues

- **Issue**: Wi-Fi dropping intermittently or difficulty connecting to networks.

- **Solution**:

  o **Restart Router**: Power cycle your router by unplugging it for 30 seconds, then plugging it back in.

  o **Forget Network**: Go to Settings > Wi-Fi, tap on the network name, and select "Forget This Network." Reconnect by entering the Wi-Fi password.

  o **Reset Network Settings**: Go to Settings > General > Reset > Reset Network Settings. Note that this will reset all Wi-Fi, Bluetooth, and VPN settings.

3. App Crashes or Freezes

- **Issue**: Apps crashing or freezing unexpectedly.

- **Solution**:
  - o **Update Apps**: Ensure all apps are updated to the latest versions available on the App Store.
  - o **Restart or Force Close**: Double-click the Home button (for devices with the Home button) or swipe up from the bottom of the screen (for devices without the Home button) to access the App Switcher. Swipe up on the app's preview to force close it.
  - o **Delete and Reinstall**: Delete the problematic app and reinstall it from the App Store.

4. Performance Issues

- **Issue**: Sluggish performance or lagging interface response.
- **Solution**:
  - o **Clear Storage**: Free up storage space by deleting unnecessary files, photos, or videos.
  - o **Reduce Motion**: Go to Settings > Accessibility > Motion and turn on "Reduce Motion" to minimize animations and effects that may affect performance.
  - o **Disable Background App Refresh**: Go to Settings > General > Background App Refresh and turn it off for apps that do not require background updates.

5. Touchscreen Responsiveness

- **Issue**: Touchscreen not responding or responding intermittently.
- **Solution**:
  - o **Clean Screen**: Clean the touchscreen with a soft, lint-free cloth to remove dirt or residue that may interfere with touch sensitivity.
  - o **Restart Device**: Restart your device to refresh the system and resolve temporary issues affecting touchscreen responsiveness.
  - o **Check for Updates**: Ensure iOS and all apps are up to date to avoid compatibility issues affecting touchscreen performance.

6. App Compatibility

- **Issue**: Apps not functioning properly or displaying compatibility warnings.

- **Solution**:

  o **Update Apps**: Update all apps to their latest versions available on the App Store to ensure compatibility with iOS 18.

  o **Check Developer Updates**: Visit the app developer's website or support page for any announcements or updates regarding iOS 18 compatibility.

  o **Contact Developer**: If an app continues to have issues, contact the app developer for assistance or report the problem through the App Store.

7. System Updates

- **Issue**: Unable to download or install iOS updates.

- **Solution**:

  o **Check Internet Connection**: Ensure a stable Wi-Fi connection or use cellular data (if applicable) with sufficient signal strength.

  o **Restart and Retry**: Restart your device and try downloading the update again through Settings > General > Software Update.

  o **iTunes Update**: Connect your device to a computer with iTunes and update iOS using iTunes if over-the-air updates fail.

www.ingramcontent.com/pod-product-compliance
Lightning Source LLC
Chambersburg PA
CBHW071256050326
40690CB00011B/2414